THE LAST SAILORMAN

THE LAST SAILORMAN

by

Dick Durham

TERENCE DALTON LIMITED
LAVENHAM . SUFFOLK
1989

Published by
TERENCE DALTON LIMITED

ISBN 0 86138 067 3

Text photoset in 10/11 pt Baskerville

Printed in Great Britain at
The Lavenham Press Limited, Lavenham, Suffolk

Contents

Acknowledgements

I WOULD like to thank the following people for spending the time to remember:-

Sheila Roberts, the late Arthur "Bully" Bull, Anne Roberts, Jill Bennett, Frances Ayton, Harry Bottreill, Sheila Trefusis, John Bell, the late Jerry Thomason, Bert Fry, Ken Fry, the late Jimmy Uglow, Phillip "Ginger" Latham, Maurice "Banger" Everett, Jimmy Penn, Jack "Blondie" Woods, the late Jack Nunn, Dave Kennard, the late Hervey Benham, Billy Evans, John Dickens, Fred "Bimbo" Mackie, Christopher Pritchard-Barrett, Paddy O'Donnell, May Quantrill, Ivan Hazelton, George Dray, Paddy O'Driscoll, Albert Butterfant, Des Sleightholme, Ron Turner, Lewis Fordyce, Jack Govier, Peter Sharman, John Haig, Arthur Wakelin, Marion Corney, Fred Jordan, Harry Boreham, Henry Parsons, Billy Willis, Walter Bartleman, Bertie Joliffe, Maisie Farley, Biddy Smart, George "Ikky" Drakes, and Tony Farnham.

For my mother Nancy

Author's Preface

ON SATURDAY, 17th October, 1970, the great gates of Tilbury Docks swung slowly shut, segregating its pond from the swirling waters of the River Thames and sealing off for ever the era of sail.

It was a mild afternoon; only the hazy light hinted at summer's imminent demise. *Cambria's* russet tops'l curved to the breeze as she set off to deliver the last cargo to be carried under sail in Great Britain and northern Europe.

Two hundred years before, bargemen had been christened "sailormen" in the London docks to distinguish them from lightermen who manoeuvred dumb barges. At the wheel of the *Cambria* was the last of them—Bob Roberts.

Further for'ard, at the brails winch letting out the big bellying mainsail, was myself, who had the distinction of being the last mate to trade under sail.

Curled up on the hatches was Penny the border collie.

A man, a boy and a dog.

Bob Roberts and his lurcher Dusty, a predecessor of Penny the border collie, aboard *Cambria* in Yarmouth harbour, photographed by Clifford Temple.

Tony Farnham collection

CHAPTER ONE

The Bicycle Ride

THE HILL looked harmless enough; it supported a farmer's home and the sticky, ploughed fields of his labours. Naked winter elms hung over it and grubby hedgerows escorted a lane out of the village and up over its back.

The catch came in its gradient.

Bob Roberts did not immediately notice the lane beneath his bicycle wheels beginning to climb. His huge hands, crudely efficient at gathering thrashing canvas in a gale, looked odd dominating the handlebars of a lady's bicycle. There was a smile of reassurance on his face.

Up ahead riding as passenger in his wife's car was a man who appeared to have a deal going with Father Time.

Bob chuckled. Old Arthur Wakelin, a retired miner, who after fifty-two years down a Midlands pit had come to give his lungs a breather in the Isle of Wight, had been out celebrating St Valentine's Day—just two days hence—with a lady friend. Arthur was eighty-six and Bob was impressed. Here was a man twelve years Bob's senior behaving like a horny teenager. With dreamy indulgence Bob comforted himself; eighty-six was a long way off yet.

Old Arthur always got off his daughter's bike just after the stone bridge where the lane started to rise. Frequently his journeys home from the Conservative Club in the village of Alverstone terminated in the hedge. The hospitality of those who had retired into politics was bounded only by closing-time.

On this still, sunny February day in 1982 Arthur was returning home from his Cupid's mission when he excavated another hole in the hedge. He was still sitting, slightly dazed, at the side of the road when Bob and Sheila drove round a bend and came across him. His bike was jammed in the hedge and as they went to his assistance Arthur told them of his St Valentine outing. Bob was delighted with this old man's hoary libido and offered to preserve it by giving him a lift home. Bob would ride his bike while Sheila drove him in the car.

It was an accident, stumbling across Arthur. They had left their home in

Captain Bob Roberts.   *Mrs Sheila Roberts*

1

Ryde with some rubbish for a nearby dump and had taken the wrong turning.

By the time this incongruous convoy reached the hill Arthur was wide awake again, refreshed from the manic licking and ear-splitting barking of Bob's border collies, Stormy and Jenny.

Arthur turned to Sheila and said, "That hill's steeper than it looks."

She stopped the car. Bob wobbled up and put his arm on the roof. Sheila passed on the warning.

Bob laughed and assured her he would take it steadily. Fancy old Arthur having a Valentine at eighty-six.

Sheila drove off up the hill, watching Bob in the driving-mirror.

He was fooling about, weaving the bike, taking his feet off the pedals and waving those mighty fists—look no hands!

It was the last time she saw him alive.

 Sailing vessels lying at Poole quay. *Robert Malster*

CHAPTER TWO

A Polite Profession

I N SUMMER the perfect reflection of the big, black-sided ships was wrinkled only when swans swam across the surface of Poole Harbour. In the airless heat the drying square-sails of brigantines and barquentines hung limp and mildewed. It was the early nineteen-twenties, and though steam had taken over on the ocean routes sail still retained a place in the coastal trade. Bob sat on the coolness of the cast-iron bollards, watching.

In winter the relentless south-westerly winds blew the smell of tarred rigging and sweet yellow timber into his face. The yards hung above his head over the quay, creaking as the men hauled out the cargo. Timber from the Baltic was stacked on the quayside. The main export was clay from the harbour's Isle of Purbeck.

What caught Bob's imagination were the men who manned these wind-machines. It fascinated him the way they strode along the quay with their knuckles facing forward. He fancied it was in readiness to grab a rope. During his school holidays he could cycle the six miles from his village, Ferndown, a downhill ride most of the way to Poole.

The uphill struggle home really started when Bob got indoors. His schoolmaster father, Albert, had other ideas for his only son. Going to sea in a sailing ship was a dead-end job as far as he was concerned. Any career reliant on muscle-power had a future which would wither with physical decline.

Albert noticed how Bob always aligned himself ancestrally with his mother. Her family, the Kings and the Browns, were dotted along the bleak shingle shores of Kessingland in Suffolk. Among their ranks were boatbuilders, fishermen and lifeboatmen. Bob was quite definite about it, he had more of his mother Annie in him than he had of his father.

His grand-uncle Louis Brown, for example, had gone to the Arctic in the *Diane* on one of the relief expeditions searching for John Franklin. Louis had been round the world several times on sailing ships and Bob loved to hear the story of grand-uncle Louis's remark to a young bargeman he once met in a Lowestoft pub. The eager bargeman proudly described his voyage up from London and his skilful negotiation of the sandbanks en route. Then he asked Louis whether or not he had ever been to London. Louis's reply had been one of the verbal heirlooms handed down in living room banter with great pleasure until it sparked off young Bob Roberts.

"Yes, boy, I've been to London, but when we went there we used to have to go round the world first."

Albert wanted his son in a profession, a "polite" profession. Bob had a chorister's scholarship from his grammar school to attend the ancient Wimborne Minster. In the hope that this scholarship would lead him to Oxford University his mother played down her family's salt-sodden veins. She kept quiet about grand-uncle Louis and instead told Bob, "You must keep on with your schooling and pass your examinations."

Both Albert and Annie hoped Bob would take his Oxford Senior Examination.

It was better when Bob played with his sisters Doris and Frances; girls could not go to sea. Frances, known always as Cis, was two years older than Bob and often looked after him when they were children. Albert approved of this although he never realised she became Bob's most trusted confidante and a willing ear to his sea fever. People thought Bob and Cis were twins. Once they went to a fancy dress party as the Bisto Kids.

During the family outings to Bournemouth Bob spent most of his time on the pier. Out on the horizon in the summer mist he could see the white cliffs of the Needles. The silhouettes of sailing craft were etched clearly against them. Cis would amuse herself by sticking a halfpenny stamp down on the boards of the pier. She tried to divert Bob's attention by pointing out the passers-by who surreptitiously attempted to pick it up.

Bob was bored with family picnics. He was becoming more interested in a family friend called George Cridland. George had a boat.

George had a profound effect on young Bob. He took him sailing in his twenty-six-foot yacht *Ariel*. She had no engine. Once they watched a power yacht drift alongside Poole Bar Buoy after it had broken down. George told Bob: "If you can't sail a boat into harbour you shouldn't leave harbour". Bob started talking about going to sea. His father, Pop as he was always called, thought things were getting desperate. In an effort to get closer to his son he once rowed to the Isle of Wight with him. Unfortunately he was seasick and Bob was not impressed.

Pop did not fit in with the image Bob was beginning to form of himself. He loved his father, but the man who was headmaster at the village school and who had previously been a teacher at St Mary's College in Caernarfon did not have the pedigree that interested Bob. Years later Bob would refer to his father in vague terms: "He was at sea to begin with, but gave it up early in life."

Apparently Pop taught seamanship briefly on a school-ship at Saltash on the Tamar. This relatively small part of his career was emphasised by Bob.

All his time outside school Bob spent down at the quay. He watched the sailors crumpling squeezeboxes outside the *Poole Arms*, known by them as "the

4

Poole harbour in the days of sailing vessels. *Robert Malster*

toilet" because of its green, glazed tile front. With their beery shanties and step-dances on the cobbles Bob fancied they saw people bound by *terra firma* as inferior. He told George: "Some of them have been round the Horn. They are real men who despise office clerks. I want to be one of them."

The message was passed on to Pop, who then made inquiries with the P & O Line and the Royal Mail at Southampton. If he could not stop his son going to sea he would at least make sure it was with an engine under him, a future before him, but he could not afford to send his son to sea as an apprentice. There would be tropical uniforms to buy, and spending money.

When Bob was almost fifteen, Pop lost him to a sailing ship. Bob was down at Poole Quay as usual coveting the grunting sailors' work aboard the barquentine *Waterwitch*, unloading coal from Goole. Bob became transfixed by her bowsprit lifting up and down on the gentle swell. He asked the mate, a Cornishman named Bert Garravick,

"Can I come and stand on your deck?"

Once aboard he never forgot the thrill of movement as the *Waterwitch* heaved up and down like a sleeping man's chest. He imagined himself rounding the Horn, as he later told Cis. His reverie was broken when the mate asked him if he wanted to go to sea. They were short of a cabin lad. The ship was discharging for another three days but Bob signed on immediately, without consulting his

5

The barquentine *Water-witch* at anchor in Falmouth, 1923.
Tony Farnham collection

parents first. When he got home he explained to his shocked mother that the ship was only going down to Fowey in Cornwall to load china clay.

"Well, you can come back from Fowey then," she said.

At Fowey Bob was handed a shovel and told to help trim the clay under the decks in the hold. As soon as the *Waterwitch* finished loading she set sail for Liverpool, with Bob still aboard. As he later explained, the ship had to save her tide. Not only that, there was another ship waiting to take her berth.

Once under way Bob was given the disappointing task of greasing the ship's store of eggs to keep them fresh. He wanted a rope to haul on, not a galley job. He devised a way of getting the job finished quickly in the hope of being included in the more manly task of sailing the ship. He melted the grease and dipped the shells in the warm mess. Later it was discovered that Bob's expediency had provided the crew with ready-cooked eggs.

His worried parents received a short note from Bob when the ship docked. It read: "Ship didn't stop—so am in Liverpool." He eventually came home from Falmouth after the *Waterwitch* had discharged coal at the gasworks there.

At Poole again, Bob looked despondently at the "Back To School" signs in

6

the windows of the children's outfitters. He was to spend another year at Wimborne Grammar. Pop got his own way when Bob left. He was placed in a chemist shop in Bournemouth to learn the alchemy of pharmacopoeia. Bob cycled to and from his job. He argued with his parents and eventually walked out of the chemist shop, only to be railroaded into an office job with an estate agent.

The cane Pop kept in the corner of the parlour held little fear for Bob, who was growing into a natural athlete. Annie could foresee the inevitable: Bob's deep chest and powerful arms looked pretty redundant in such sedentary work. Nevertheless his strapping physique was a boon to his new employers. Collecting rents from their properties was one aspect of an otherwise dull job in which Bob excelled. The once-reluctant tenants pushed their cash through the letter box rather than face the lantern-jawed youngster when he called.

The job did not last and by the age of seventeen Bob was back at sea on a West Country schooner.

While in Calais loading pit props and boulders to be crushed for pottery powder Bob's seafaring days almost came to a premature end. The vessel was waiting to lock out, bound for a Welsh port. At the top end of the dock was a much bigger Norwegian schooner. Bob and his mates watched in amazement as the ship set all its canvas and came racing down towards the lock. Her skipper was drunk and late on the tide. The ship missed the lock and instead rammed her clipper bow into the smaller schooner, then, as an afterthought, dropped anchor.

Bob later told Cis: "A Norwegian anchor and thirty fathom of chain fell on our deck and nearly cut me in half."

When there was no more work for the ship she was anchored on a mud bank in Par. Bob, without his trusty bicycle, faced drawing dole money at sixteen shillings (80p) a week or a long walk round the ports to find another ship.

He set off on foot for Bridport, some hundred miles away. On the way he lived on the proceeds of odd jobs he picked up. For a publican he killed a goose by clubbing it with a lump of wood. He washed glasses, swept up, and carried on to Bridport with thirty shillings (£1.50) jangling in his pocket.

When he reached Bridport there was no berth. He was advised to try London.

He set off once again. At Ringwood in Hampshire he was attracted by the glow of a brazier belonging to a nightwatchman. The man worked with a road-mending gang and he gave Bob some tea. He spent the night in his warm caravan and the following day changed course for Bournemouth. The nightwatchman promised Bob a cut of his previous unemployment pay which he had not collected and could not now do so for fear of losing his job. Bob took a note of authority from the man and duly returned with £3. With his cut Bob set off yet again and stopped at a farm where he earned his board by sawing up a pile of logs.

He eventually arrived on a farm near Bromley in Kent and, because he could count, Bob found himself operating a pair of scales weighing strawberries picked by gipsies. When the gipsy women urinated on the dry earth and then rubbed their strawberry baskets in the resulting slush to increase their "yield" Bob treated the matter philosophically. The fruit was going for jam anyway, be reasoned.

On this farm Bob was put in charge of feeding and cleaning two big shire horses which worked the fields. He had to be up at 3 am to tend the shires and on the first morning he stumbled bleary-eyed into the stables. He had forgotten the instructions given him the day before: if he ran his hand along the side of the animal, then down the leg, the beast would lift its foot for the fetlocks to be cleaned. Bob grabbed the first ankle he found in the dim light and yanked at it. The great horse kicked free and stamped on the ground in disgust, narrowly missing Bob's head.

With thirty-five shillings (£1.75) a week coming in and living on a diet of fruit Bob saved £7. One day he spotted an advertisement for a reporter with an Orpington newspaper. He had shown an early talent for writing and also remembered enjoying the task of listing and describing the properties during his time with the estate agent. This job seemed an easy way to make some quick cash. He got it, but he soon found flower shows and weddings tiresome events to describe. To liven things up he once let a local farmer's cows out of his field and filed a report on the event. He gained some experience sub-editing before leaving the paper, fearing he might become too flabby and weak for a seaman's life. During this brief interlude he had raised his parents' hopes again.

He arrived in London and when walking down Blackfriars Road he noticed a group of about twenty fit young men holding brown paper parcels standing outside an odd rectangular-shaped building. It was The Ring, a converted chapel where young boxers punched the guts out of each other for two shillings and sixpence (12½p) a round.

When a white-haired, white moustachioed man came out of the building fights broke out among the crowd of young men. Bob discovered their brown parcels held boxing gloves and shorts. The white-haired man was the manager, George Harris, who had come out to call for some fighters. There was more boxing to be seen in the street outside than there was inside, such was the competition to get in.

Bob was fit enough to fight and lean and hungry enough to need the money, but by the time the manager had taken his cut and the men who sponged him down, the seconds, had taken theirs Bob fully understood the reason why The Ring had failed as a place of worship. Previous congregations, it was said, had thought the eight-sided building had too many corners for the devil to hide in.

CHAPTER THREE

Shipshape—Erith Fashion

WHERE the London River sweeps south round Coldharbour Point and into Erith Rands there is a forgotten semicircle of saltings. This bight of flora, as yet unexploited by encroaching heavy industry, is where Bob set off on the most ambitious voyage he was ever to make.

He had found digs in St Mary Cray while looking for a berth in a ship. Instead of getting away to sea he ran into a young man called Dick Crowhurst who was a member of a yacht club based on a leaky old barge at Erith called the *Garson*, an old boomie built at Great Yarmouth in 1864. The club house of the Erith Yacht Club was reached by a curious walkway of old hatch-boards, driftwood and wrecked boat planking across the marshes. There was a ramp similarly constructed with rail tracks nailed to it. The whole affair looked like some obsolete open-cast mining town.

There was a peculiar smell to the River as well, hard to define, but somehow it was of metal, of what could be done to it and of what it could do. All around the skyline, blackened factory chimneys belched smoke into the reeking atmosphere.

The illustrious history of such an uninspiring blot impressed Bob. It was here that the Royal Corinthian Yacht Club, now based at Burnham-on-Crouch, was founded in 1893 and from here that the first Thames sailing barge race was organised by Henry Dodd, the waste disposal millionaire known as the "Golden Dustman".

Bob had doubts at first about associating with yachtsmen. They were not professionals after all. But Dick and another massively built yachtsman, Arthur "Bully" Bull, were more likely to be spattered in river mud than dripping in gold braid. Bob saw the potential of the no-airs-and-graces club and its members. It was the right base to plan an ocean voyage.

Bob had long spells out of work. He managed to get occasional shifts sub-editing the sports pages of the *Daily Mail* but he could equally find himself potato picking. Already he was working to a regime to enable him to save for a boat that would take him round the world. He kept his plan mainly to himself, letting on to most people that he was intending only to make an Atlantic crossing.

In an eighteen-foot sloop, the *Tern*, which he bought for £25 to learn small-boat sailing, Bob used the Thames Estuary to practise coastal navigation.

He practised his hand-bearing compass on anything that offered itself, including a low-flying German Zeppelin.

His first sailing companion was Frank Lucy, who had a fair knowledge of navigation. He was useful in another way, too. When Bob got hard up he eventually moved from his digs and slept in the wireless shop Frank rented near Orpington Station.

Once Bob and another friend, Lewis Fordyce, were bound for Ramsgate in thick fog. They ran aground on Kingsgate rocks and spent the night lying over at forty-five degrees after the tide went out. The little vessel had room for a gramophone and while Lewis fried bacon and eggs the following morning to the harmony of *I'm Crying for the Carolines*, Bob attempted to fix their position. "According to my reckoning we're four mile sou'-west of Leeds," he said.

Interspersed with these short trips Bob read all the accounts of small boat voyaging he could lay hands on. E. F. Knight in particular influenced him. He admired Knight's unsentimental attitude to his crew and his "macho" sportsmanship in trolling for what Knight referred to as "Mr Shark".

One morning the *Tern* lay in the quiet backwater of Havengore, her planking rippling on the flood tide. Bob, Frank and Lewis were preparing to sail back to Erith when they noticed the riding light had fallen overboard. Bob, who had learned from his reading the importance of taking firm decisions as Master, ordered Lewis over the side to find it. However, a cursory look round would have sufficed. After swimming about under the water, Lewis eventually bumped into the riding light which was swaying in the current ten feet astern of the boat, still attached to its cable.

Equally Bob knew it was the skipper's responsibility to see his ship did not founder. Thus, one cold, wet and windy March night while sailing back from Margate he did not hesitate to jump over the side to push the boat clear when they ran on to the Blyth Sands. This time Lewis had the pleasure of remaining dry and also out of range of his skipper's language, for Bob was also the navigator.

These jolly jaunts were only the run up to the big adventure, and for that Bob needed another man with time to spare and without a profession, "polite" or otherwise. Lewis was starting a career in the Army, Frank drifted away.

Bully was almost a head taller than Bob, his shoulders, chest and arms were the imposing foundation for a neck that could have been used as a bollard. The City of London Police had thought so too, and Bully, after three years as a mechanic in a Chislehurst garage, was feeling collars in the Metropolis. Bob and Bully had become good friends. Bully had kept back half his dinner for Bob when Bob was really hard up, with nothing left to pawn. Bully was living at home and Bob crept into the garden shed at night to sleep. However, there was one thing that strongly divided them. Engines. Bully was bewitched by the speed mechanical contraptions promised. Bob dismissed his enthusiasm as a bad habit.

By now Bob had progressed from his compass and dividers and was learning how to use the sextant. He had sold the *Tern* and was saving for the boat which he hoped would take him round the world. He cycled everywhere to save money, gave up smoking and even cut his own hair to save for the cause.

It was now the talk of the yacht club that Bully planned to go along with Bob. He was not involved in the purchase of the boat but Bob expected him to show a sense of responsibility towards victualling and preparing generally for the trip. Therefore they had a furious row when Bully, still on his policeman's pay, indulged his love of speed in a Norton 8. Whistling along the roads on this beloved motorcycle, the generous-hearted Bully would often stop to help motorists who had broken down. Frequently this led to his late arrival for sailing trips with Bob and consequently to further arguments.

The *Thelma*, a twenty-seven-foot gaff cutter, was the vessel Bob paid for out of his hard-earned savings in 1930 and which was to realise his dream, or nearly. She made two trial voyages, this time further afield than Burnham, Margate and Ramsgate. The first was a three-week round trip from Erith to Le Havre, Poole, Brixham, Torquay, Ramsgate and back to Erith. Bob, Dick Crowhurst and Bully

Bob Roberts and Arthur "Bully" Bull after winning a marathon for Cambridge Harriers in the nineteen-twenties.
Mrs Sheila Roberts

11

made the trip, and Bob's original uncertainty about the yachting fraternity was personified in Torquay harbour. Tied up alongside the polished topsides of sparkling yachts and dazzled by the brass-buttoned reefers, the unshaven crew of the *Thelma* felt somewhat inhibited. But not for long.

Bob noted in his log: "Tied up alongside the highbrows of Torquay. Ship, skipper and crew are all a hopeless misfit. We have no Oxford accent; we drink common beer instead of wines; we do our own singing instead of having a wireless (especially after the aforesaid beer). There's going to be a general exit of Torquay society if we stay another day."

During the second trial voyage, a twenty days round trip to Germany and Holland, Bully mentioned to Bob while they were becalmed the value of having an auxiliary motor. Bob ignored him and practised taking midday sunsights.

Sailing into the Ems-Jade canal, the *Thelma* collided with a motor barge. The *Thelma* had right of way but the boy at the wheel of the barge put the helm over the wrong way when the skipper shouted at him. They sustained no damage but as *Thelma's* crew watched the skipper chasing the boy with a spanner, Bob's unstated belief in the superiority of wind over power seemed to be backed up by fate itself.

It was a wonder Bully ever set sail with Bob on the big adventure after this second trial sail. They were hove-to for twelve hours in the North Sea as a storm raged over them, blowing out the jib and splitting the mainsail. While trying to get some sleep on the cabin floor Bully suffered a bash on the head from a falling clock. In April, 1933, the pair were finally ready to set sail. Bob had his last meal ashore at the home of his old friend Lewis, or rather he had his last look at a meal ashore. The roast lamb cutlets and apple pie were too much for someone whose dedication to his voyage had included a fanatical diet of hard-tack.

Apart from the members of Erith Yacht Club only one other person knew of the epic voyage about to start. A few days before setting sail Bob had written to Cis. "Pop might try and stop me going away, Cis. But you know it wouldn't do any good. I don't want him to worry so keep this a secret. I'll be in touch."

CHAPTER FOUR

Wind of Escape

B ULLY lay dozing on the coach-roof in the sun. He was exhausted and trying to dream himself off the ship and away from the last few days of violent seasickness. As the *Thelma* rolled in the dying swell her sails slatted against the rigging and brought him back from his sixty-miles-per-hour motorcycle ride down a straight country road to the windless, watery wastes of the English Channel.

They were at the tail end of an easterly gale which had dragged *Thelma* down the Channel from Poole in two days. They had both been soaked through, both been cold, and the two-hour watches they were keeping were worse for Bully who was finding his sea-legs slow growing. Since the week they had spent fitting out and taking on stores at Poole Bully had consumed only cheese, biscuits and Bovril. Bob had little sympathy for him. As well as standing his own watch, he was cooking, making up the bunks, and trimming and filling the lamps in between working out his sun sights. This hyperactive industry was a hint Bully understood, but the resulting guilt made him perversely more stubborn. He felt slightly hurt that the sickness which had weakened his huge frame should be ignored. Bob's insensitivity was a controlled way of showing his anger. He refused to acknowledge anything that might jeopardise the voyage.

Bob thought about the Cornishman he had met in a Poole bar. Most nights Bully went to the cinema while Bob frequented the quayside pubs. In one he met an interesting old seaman with only one hand. He had lost the other during his days as a wrecker on the Cornish coast. He told Bob they would leave some of their pickings from the unfortunate vessels driven ashore on the cliffside to satisfy the coastguards they had so recently fled. Meanwhile they would hide their ill-gotten gains in caves, ulletts as they were called, until the coast was clear. One of these characters had dragged some large heavy object into an ullett one night and guarded it until daylight. As the first rays of dawn lit the cavern the wrecker realised he had dragged the corpse of a drowned sailor into his lair. He had to wait all day until nightfall and then drag the corpse back to the water's edge. This time he was spotted by coastguards. He got away with a yarn that he had just "rescued" the stiff from the water.

Seven days out from Poole the *Thelma* was still rolling badly in a cross sea as she wallowed across the Bay of Biscay. Bully had found his sea-legs at last and he and Bob ate meals of mackerel fried in lard. The bait was rind from bacon which Bob noted had cost them eleven pence (5p) a pound.

Chafe became a problem, and much of the time the *Thelma* had her mainsail lowered to prevent wear and tear. Bully spent hours making chafing gear from old ropes. Meanwhile Bob's confidence in his navigation increased. After taking sun sights one morning he noted: "Very fascinating to take a couple of squints at the sun and say 'Land, show thyself'. When the land obeys I feel that I have almost worked a miracle."

The *Thelma* berthed alongside Vigo pier thirteen days out from Poole. Here the pair met a German stowaway called Max who came from Danzig. He had sneaked on to a ship bound for Buenos Aires but was discovered and put ashore at the Spanish port.

They spent hours ashore drinking wine and listening to the big, broad-shouldered, fair-haired German. He impressed them with his knowledge of history, and the pair listened to theories which less than a decade later would

The Thelma in the Thames off Erith before leaving on her long voyage.   *Mrs Sheila Roberts*

The *Thelma* at Erith.
Mrs Sheila Roberts

shock the world. Bob wrote: "He makes a study of racial diversions. A Hitlerite in theory, he believes that eventually all the Nordic races—English, German, Dutch and Scandinavian—must unite before they become ruled by the southerners and yellow people."

Both Bully and Bob found the delights of shore life irritating because they had not the money to enjoy them. Consequently they decided not to explore Lisbon, their next port of call, and spent only a morning ashore there before setting sail for Gibraltar.

Gibraltar was different; it was British. They moored north of the Rock, surrounded by the fuss and bustle of a hundred craft. Launches, tugs, lighters and fishing boats swarmed round the *Thelma* day and night. There was even a battered old fishing smack running contraband tobacco from Gibraltar to Spain. British or not, the narrow streets of Gibraltar were most cosmopolitan. Bob, remembering Max's warning, noted: "Trading in the town we found Englishmen, Spaniards, Moors, Arabs, Indians, Portuguese, Frenchmen, Italians, Maltese and even a Malay."

Bob, having watched a bullfight in Algeciras, convinced himself the national sport symbolised dago faint-heartedness. Both he and Bully found the spectacle cruel. They were both fond of animals and Bob carried childhood memories of the working horses in his village. The sight of the blindfolded horses carrying the picadors being battered by furious bulls angered Bob. He concluded: "My idea of a bullfight would be to put the matador and the bull into the ring together (without any of the foreplay), and if the matador cannot make a kill in say half an hour or so, let it be said that the beast is victorious and has won his freedom. It would certainly be a fairer fight. The Spaniard praises the

15

bullfighter for his nerve and daring but all the tricks of evasion and side-stepping are from what I could observe only a matter of practice. Anyone with any pluck at all could become a matador."

Bob and Bully fell out in Gibraltar when Bully dropped a marlinespike over the side and later lost the bucket to the deeps. Bob swore at him and Bully refused to eat his dinner and went ashore alone, but before they left the port the pair went ashore and settled their differences with alcohol.

A light westerly wind made things slow going for the *Thelma* as she left Gibraltar. Bully watched longingly a German ketch with an engine draw far ahead of them. He remarked on her progress to Bob. Their old argument had belched out its fumes once again, causing Bob to write in his log: "Much talk among the crew about the value of auxiliaries but we shall have to put greater value on the virtue of patience. A levanter would remedy all our trouble."

In Tangier Bob showed what a good friend he could be at sea. A British yacht, the *Gipsy*, bound for Egypt and sailed by her owner, Captain St John Smith, and his young daughter, had been beached for repainting and was being kept upright with guy ropes when one parted. She fell over on her beam ends and sprang her planking. The *Gipsy* took in water. The girl's clothing was ruined. Although all this happened around midnight, Bob and Bully turned out and offered the girl a berth aboard the *Thelma* while they spent the rest of the night trying to clear things up.

Without knowing what lay in store for the *Thelma*, Bob wrote: "We pottered about and helped where we could but I thanked my stars it wasn't us who were in such an unholy mess."

Three days out of Tangier the *Thelma* picked up the trade wind and a fair current which uplifted Bob, so much so that he started praising Bully, who since the bullfight had been re-christened Toro. After two months together Bob wrote: "Bully is becoming a better sailor every day." They talked about everything as the *Thelma* splashed along in the sun, her large squaresail pulling her through the sparkling blue sea. Bob's love of history made him an interesting companion. His interest had been fired when a highwayman's boot was discovered in the attic of his old grammar school. Bully talked mainly of engineering, but in such idyllic conditions Bob listened politely.

These two young men from a muddy yacht club were skimming along in the sun about to enter the Atlantic. Unmarried, free as birds, on a sailing adventure their companions back at Erith could only dream of.

The exhilaration they felt naturally made them closer. Bully's clumsiness and seasickness and Bob's demanding, sometimes unreasonable, captaincy were forgotten. The shipmates started planning to buy a schooner with which to earn a living. As the *Thelma* creamed along with a cracking fair wind, overtaken only by flying fish, Bully's mechanical soul became aware of the beauty of the earth's own engine, its convection machine. With such easy watches Bob imagined Bully

Bob Roberts taking a sun sight for latitude during *Thelma's* passage from Tangier to Tenerife.
Mrs Sheila Roberts

as a first-rate hand. They agreed to try to buy a schooner of fifty to eighty tons. She would be crewed by the old faithfuls back home, including Dick Crowhurst.

They trimmed the sheets until the *Thelma* sailed herself while they lay on deck in the sun. Bob wrote: "This cruise wouldn't be much cop without Bully. He is becoming a better seaman every day now and his quaint touch of humour combined with a bland, phlegmatic outlook on everything in general makes him an ideal partner to go adventuring with." As the *Thelma's* anchor splashed down into the harbour of Santa Cruz de Tenerife a small motor launch was setting out from the shore. It was the British consul, who came out to greet them officially and towed them to a berth off the yacht club. They were invited ashore to attend a dance at the club. Things looked promising. Sex had been another of the subjects the shipmates had discussed in their two months afloat, and some of the ladies at the club were bored with island life.

Bob and Bully shaved and spruced themselves up but were pretty crestfallen when the German barman at the club told them shirtsleeves was not the correct way to dress. Disgusted at such pomposity they went back aboard the *Thelma* and played cards!

Social activity revolved around the yacht club, but Bob was more interested in the local political unrest. The British consul told the two voyagers how he had been set upon one night by rioters who forced him to repeat "Long live the

Republic", but when they tried to force him also to utter "Die the monarchy" he punched one of the rioters and the ensuing brawl was stopped by the Civil Guard.

The thought of a punch-up, especially if it could be justified by defence of the crown, any crown, appealed to Bob but he did not get the chance. Instead the island life, or lack of it, caused him to comment: "Life ashore here is pretty stagnant. Everyone knows everyone and is somewhat sick of the sight of everyone. The numerous members of the yacht club come down to swim in the morning, again in the afternoon and in the evening they just lounge about—fed up and bored to tears. They all seem anxious to set foot in England again at the earliest possible moment."

As children swarmed all over the *Thelma's* rigging the well-dressed killjoys of the Club Nautico warned the British yachtsmen that their intended landfall on the other side of the Atlantic, Georgetown, had just experienced a severe cyclone. And on only their second day out both Bully and Bob were badly affected by some contaminated drinking water they had taken aboard at Tangier. In their enfeebled state they broke the main boom in two as they lowered the mainsail to prevent wear from slatting.

Bully took to his bunk and Bob lay weak and listless on the floor of the cockpit as the *Thelma* sailed along under jib alone. Both were too sick to set any more sail. Bob wrote: "No passage ever started with more ominous forebodings."

Bob and Bully enjoying a frugal meal during their transatlantic passage. They found that by eating less they did not feel so much the craving for water. *Mrs Sheila Roberts*

CHAPTER FIVE

Treasure Island

B ULLY's seamanship increased in direct proportion to the Beaufort Scale. The burly former policeman did not have the concentration to capitalise on the subtle wind changes during light airs. Therefore, during the airless days of the *Thelma's* Atlantic crossing, Bob was vexed by Bully's steering and consequently fretted about their dwindling food stocks. Conversely he cheered up during the gales, though in one storm the seas were so violent that the little cutter burst a sea anchor. He wrote: "As usual Bully's seamanship and initiative improved 50 per cent with the bad weather. If it always blew a gale of wind he could become quite a good hand."

When the wind died away Bob counted the food stocks and worked out emergency rationing. It never became necessary to implement rationing, however, and a typical day's diet was breakfast: flying fish and chips; dinner: tinned salmon, boiled potatoes and gherkins, bananas, cheese and biscuits; supper: porridge.

On his twenty-sixth birthday Bob was worrying about finances. "Been wondering lately if we'll be able to make the complete trip round the world. The main factors are how much it's going to cost to get through the Panama Canal, how long funds will last and how long the boat will remain seaworthy without any expensive repairs."

Totting up his savings Bob found he had £12 banked in England, £100 in a building society plus a further £146 in a letter of credit. Bully had £35 in cash. In mid-Atlantic Bob started dreaming up ideas to feed the gold mine he had already experienced—Fleet Street. He wrote: "Must set to and write like hell when we get to Georgetown. Have been thinking out some ideas for an article for the *Daily Mail*. Something along these lines: 'I often wonder what my editor would think if he could see one of his late 'subs' steering a sailing vessel before an Atlantic gale, stripped to the waist and with three weeks' growth of hair on his chin, one hand grasping the kicking helm while the other performed acrobatics with a saucepan full of steaming porridge.

"'I often wonder too what Lord Trenchard would think if he could see one of his constables of four months ago wedged in our diminutive galley frying fish and chips to the accompaniment of a stream of vituperation.'

"That's all tripe I know, but it's the sort of stuff that goes down." He was right. That story was eventually used word for word.

On board *Thelma* on the way through the Panama Canal.
Mrs Sheila Roberts

Fifty days out Bully spotted a butterfly. After sounding he found there were sixteen fathoms of water below the *Thelma*. Later he and Bob made out hazy chimney stacks of the sugar factories on the low-lying coast of British Guiana (now known as Guyana). The *Thelma* had crossed the Atlantic. The little white ship had been observed by the coastguards who manned the Demerara Beacon standing nine miles offshore. The *Thelma* moored to the beacon's staging and the shipmates were brought tea. As they chatted with a pilot who was waiting for a steamer, police were on their way downriver expecting to arrest two escaped prisoners from the legendary Devil's Island. The beacon men had wirelessed to shore to report that two half-naked men with long beards had arrived with some ridiculous story about having sailed from London. Only after much cursing and waving of Bills of Health and passports was the *Thelma* was allowed to proceed to Georgetown.

Throughout the West Indies it was hard to believe that sail power was becoming obsolete. In every harbour and between every island sails flecked the glittering water. In Port of Spain, Trinidad, Bob watched schooners from Barbados, Grenada and Demerara gliding in and out of the harbour. Fussing round them were myriads of sloop-rigged punts ferrying the cargo ashore.

However, at Curaçao Bob experienced first hand the throbbing future which was firstly to make him redundant and secondly to seduce him from the anachronism of merchant sail. A friendly tanker captain invited Bob and Bully aboard to witness the bridge-controlled vessel leave harbour. Bob later prophetically noted his experiences: "Instruments galore, telegraphs, mechanical precision—that is modern sailoring. No roaring mates and hours on the yard arm. No hanging on to a dipping bowsprit. No hauling and sweating on sheets and halyards. Just a few clearcut orders and the ship was under way and out to sea. The whole business of getting the ship to sea had been accomplished with scarcely a dozen words spoken. Efficiency, organisation. And people say that these steamship men should be trained in sail.

"Why? I love sailing ships, but what relation have they to the operation of a modern steamer? It is just as much sense to say that an aviator must first serve in a steamer before he can navigate an aeroplane.

"The days of sailoring are over. These men who handle steamships are not seamen in the old sense of the word. They are ordinary young men trained to do a special job and do it efficiently. Sailing ships are all right for the hard cases, the die-hards and bloody fools like me. But to teach a man to handle a steamship—put him in a steamship."

Bob questioned his own qualities, or lack of them, as a teacher of seamanship as the *Thelma* headed towards the Panama Canal. He enthused about Bully as a companion. It suited him that Bully did what he was told and never complained, but he was constantly nagging at himself over what he saw as Bully's poor seamanship.

During Bully's night watches the *Thelma* would invariably be sailing several degrees off her correct course. On one occasion Bully mistook the breaking seas on Little Curaçao reef for reflected moonlight. Bob did not have the heart to make much of it; in fact he was determined to make enough money from his writings to give Bully a share for his faithful service. Whatever doubts he had about Bully, he intended to sail round the world with the broad-shouldered companion who had kept him in the garden shed when he had nowhere else to go. Only lack of money would stop the pair in their circumnavigation attempt.

Thus at the New York Bank in Cristóbal, where they were drawing money to pay their passage through the Panama Canal, their ears pricked up when they heard about buried treasure on an island on their proposed route.

An Englishman, Hugh Craggs, told them how he had explored Cocos Island in his schooner, the *Malaya*. Craggs was an expert on the island. He had endless documents about the place, he had spent hours in the British Museum studying the uninhabited dot and he had spent forty-seven days trying to get to its centre. He told them once that it took him five hours to travel just two thirds of a mile.

It seemed a little odd, therefore, that Craggs should have told the pair that treasure was rumoured to be buried there and yet deny that there was any such loot. Ships, he told the shipmates, stopped at Cocos only to take on water after their sluggish passage through the doldrums, but it soon became clear that ships also stopped there for another reason: to find treasure.

Bob admitted in the log: "He has set us on going there."

Bob and Bully visited the Canal Zone library and read up on Cocos for themselves. They bought a .32 rifle to add to the *Thelma's* arsenal of two shotguns and a Webley pistol.

Bob's log records the fateful decision to go to Cocos: "Our idea is to go to Cocos, which is uninhabited, moor the boat safely and go exploring into the high

Thelma beached for scrubbing and painting in preparation for her voyage across the Pacific.   *Mrs Sheila Roberts*

land of the interior. Take several days' provisions, guns etc. and see what there is to be seen."

On Christmas Day an English ketch, the *Avance*, agreed to tow the *Thelma* through the Panama Canal. It seemed all the vessels of the world were being channelled through the Canal *en route* to Cocos. Another ship, the New York schooner *Franklin Barnett*, was also bound for the island. The *Avance* was manned by thirteen young men who were planning a two-year dig to find the treasure. Somehow the island's lonely charm was beginning to wear a bit thin. Bob queried: "Suppose there is treasure on Cocos and we find it while they are there?"

Despite his bleak rhetoric, he was comforted slightly at the thought of the sturdy Bully. He had been trained in weapon handling by the City of London Police.

On 22nd February, 1934, at 9 am the *Thelma* dropped anchor in Chatham Bay at the north end of Cocos Island. As the chain rattled out through the hawse they surveyed the drooping coconut palms lining the beach and climbing the mountain slopes inland. In the sweltering heat the silence was broken rather eerily by the purr of the surf on the shore. They were not alone, however. The *Franklin Barnett* was also anchored in the bay.

They called it "the coffin", the little square-shaped dinghy which had been lashed upside-down under the *Thelma's* boom. To ensure the boom would not snag they had cut the top-sides down. They rowed gingerly away from the *Thelma* watched by Jimmy Riddle, the cat they had adopted in Trinidad.

The crashing surf capsized the coffin on the beach, throwing Bob and Bully into the sea. They stepped on to the shore to be met by a skinny, round-shouldered Englishman with long red hair and a straggly beard. Bob later remarked that George Cooknell looked like Robinson Crusoe. This was hardly surprising, for Cooknell, employed by the *Franklin Barnett* crew in his profession as a metal diviner to help them find the treasure, had already fallen out with his shipmates and had set up a canvas tent of his own on the beach.

On the hill above Cooknell's tent the crew of the *Franklin Barnett*, led by her one-legged skipper Ronald Valentine, were digging for treasure. Cooknell had dug his own hole on the beach. He entertained Bully and Bob in his tent, where they both received a shock after challenging the slender Cooknell to arm wrestling. He beat them both. Digging for El Dorado had given him extra-strong arms. Cooknell told them how Cocos Island had proved a jinx on all who visited her shores. The *Avance* left after only a month with one of her crew in splints after breaking a leg and being owed £930 by his shipmates. Another vessel, the sloop *Driftwood* from New York, had also left shortly before the *Thelma's* arrival. Fist fights had broken out among her crew in their fruitless search for gold.

Thelma alongside the *Avance* in the Panama Canal. *Mrs Sheila Roberts*

23

Cooknell himself had originally been with the *Avance* but had gone ahead in the *Franklin Barnett* and beaten the other ship to the island.

Len Sinsbury and Harold Burwood, two of the crew of the *Avance*, had been left on the island to carry on the treasure hunt while awaiting the vessel's return. Needless to say there was no love lost between Cooknell and these two other would-be gold diggers.

Bob and Bully noticed the friction. Bob noted: "This damn island seems to breed discontent. Here are the quarrels going on at the moment:

"George v Valentine

"George v Stanton (*Avance*)

"George v Sinsbury and Burwood. Sinsbury v Burwood. Sinsbury and Burwood v Stanton."

The forecastle crew on the *Avance* had planned to seize the ship and sell it down in the South Sea islands, such was their disillusionment with Cocos.

Documents in the hands of the treasure seekers named Wafer Bay as being the site where part of the treasure had been buried. Both Sinsbury and Burwood were known to be in Wafer Bay. It was not surprising that Cooknell encouraged Bob and Bully to join him on an expedition to find the other men.

Armed with machetes and rifles, and with sufficient stores, the three men set off four days after the *Thelma* anchored in Chatham Bay. They were gone two days. The going had been tough, hacking through the tropical growth as Craggs had experienced. After they ran into the treasureless Sinsbury and Burwood they made the return journey to Chatham Bay in the *Avance's* lifeboat, which had been left for the men to use. Just an hour before they arrived back at Chatham Bay Ronald Valentine, who was still digging atop the hill behind the bay, noticed the *Thelma* had moved closer to the island. Wiping the sweat from his brow he peered again. There was no doubt the *Thelma* was adrift. Valentine sent two of his men down the hill with orders to do anything possible to save her, but the *Thelma* slid effortlessly and inexorably towards the breakers. There was

Thelma wrecked on the rocks of Cocos Island, which ripped out the whole of her starboard side. *Mrs Sheila Roberts*

24

no wind and she was pulled in as though fixed to a glossy sheet being rolled up by somebody on the shore. The last wave she ever rode was the one that pitched her on to the slippery, round rocks bordering the headland of Chatham Bay. She hit stern first, shearing off her rudder, then pitched round starboard side to and was punched by the booming surf into the rocks.

The long, lazy, rather sickly swell that had got up was playing on Bob's mind as he pulled in Sinsbury and Burwood's lifeboat back to Chatham Bay. He would feel better when he got round the headland and saw the *Thelma* again. When he looked out off the headland and she was not there he could hardly bear to bring his head round and look at the shore. When he did, he saw the *Thelma* with spray breaking over her, her mast juddering with every exploding breaker. They could get to her only by landing on the beach and walking round to the rocks. They saw Jimmy Riddle mewing from the masthead.

Bob, Bully and the five other men worked until midnight slithering over rocks to get what they could salvage from the *Thelma*. At first they had set out with a borrowed anchor to try to kedge her off but that was before they realised her starboard side had been torn out.

The following day they noticed about fifteen feet of chain hanging from her bow. The cable had parted. It had been made up of odd lengths and the Pacific swell had found a weak link as the *Thelma* snubbed to the seas. Bully mentioned to Bob that they should have put a weight down the chain to act as a shock absorber, but Bob did not take kindly to any useless post-mortem advice, especially of the critical kind.

He knew what Bully said might possibly have saved the *Thelma* but when he wrote his own account, published in *Rough and Tumble*, he blamed coral as having severed the three-eighth-inch chain. Yet when they anchored Bob had noted the bottom was of rock and sand.

In his log he noted that the chain had parted and then wrote: "It nearly broke my heart to see her lying there on the rocks with half her side torn out.

"Must confess that after the excitement was over I shed a tear or two. I feel inwardly thankful that she was not lost by reason of bad seamanship on my part and find some consolation that, as far as I know, her last voyage was her greatest one and brought her name out from obscurity to some degree of fame . . ."

The poignant entry, as an attempt to convince himself he was blameless, failed to work and neither Bob nor Bully mentioned the factors surrounding the *Thelma's* loss again.

Three years of preparation and a thirteen-month voyage had left Bob with a "good story" to file to the *Daily Mail*; it required little of Bob's whimsical imagination. It was that of which newspapers are made—disaster.

It was the end of the *Thelma's* round-the-world cruise. On his own, in the sun and unbeknown to Bully, Bob chiselled on what could be regarded as a suitable headstone, the rocks of Chatham Bay: "THELMA (EYC) LONDON 1934."

CHAPTER SIX

The Black Schooner

A T NIGHT the tropical rain combined with ants and mosquitos made sleep uncomfortable on Cocos Island. At daybreak Bob and Bully swam off Chatham Bay beach to try to relieve their finger-scratched hides and came out of the water only to dodge sharks. They shot booby birds and ate them with rice. Occasionally the luxury of a wild pig would turn slowly on George Cooknell's spit.

The days dragged by. They were no longer masters of their own fate. They would have to wait until Ronald Valentine completed his "prospecting" or another ship called at the island and offered them a passage. Bully was downhearted and he was reluctant to help carry the salvaged flotsam from the *Thelma* around the rocks to the beach camp. Bob even noted that he did five trips to Bully's two. All the time Bob's thoughts were on the horizon. He wanted another boat as soon as possible and, with Bully beside him, a compass course for Tahiti. "I hope the Quarrel God of Cocos doesn't get either of us."

The Black Schooner, as Bob called the *Franklin Barnett*, eventually weighed anchor two and a half weeks after the *Thelma* was wrecked.

Bob was full of admiration for the lonely figure of George Cooknell watching them set sail from the beach. He had stayed behind, too proud to board the same ship as his gold-digging opponent. Bob gave him his shotgun and left him standing alone among the elephantine potato plants which had grown to grotesque proportions in the tropical heat.

Ronald Valentine had signed on Bob as mate and navigator and Bully as seaman. The bo'sun was a black man called Sam and the ship carried another "green" deckhand, an American called Harold Braun. Relieved of all duties was Ronald's father, known as OMV, Old Man Valentine. After twelve days' agonisingly slow progress Bob came to the conclusion that Ronald Valentine was going soft in the head. All day long he would sit in his bunk talking to himself and apparently trying to contact spirits. At night his feverish laughter could be heard echoing through the saloon. He ordered a course of due south which would put them out to sea again and which Bob delicately ignored. Often Valentine would sit in the cabin wearing the radio headphones, even though the set was not connected to the supply, which in any case had flat batteries.

Bully watched Valentine altering the chart by drawing in a new coastline for Costa Rica! Bob decided to keep the ship sailing up the Gulf of Panama until she fetched Balboa, hoping the skipper would not doubt that their position was the one he had ordered until it was too late.

Stocks of food were low and the crew lived on rice and beans. A cup of tea and a ship's biscuit was a treat. On 25th March, thirteen days from Cocos, Valentine ordered Bob to steer south-east, even though Bob reckoned they would make a Costa Rican landfall in a matter of hours. He wrote: "As it is not in my province to countermand the skipper's order (even if I do think he's a bit batty) the only thing to do is let him have his way and cancel any hopes of getting into port for another three weeks or perhaps more."

To add to the frustration of the ship's company, Sam the bo'sun was proving to be a "bucko". Bob warned him for bullying Harold Braun, the least experienced of the crew, and later Bully threatened to knock him out for teasing Jimmy Riddle.

Water was now being rationed: two gallons a day for the six of them. They fished for dolphin to eke out the food stores. They caught two dolphins and one shark, which was used not as victualling but more for the perverse pleasure of Sam. He cut off its tail and then let it go.

Against this potentially explosive background Bully went below and worked like a Trojan trying to get the seventy-horsepower engine to work. It had been out of commission since they left Cocos. Even Bob's stoic stance over engines melted into enthusiasm: "Bully was in his element today; covered with dirt and grease he set about getting the ancient engine into running order, but says it will be a long job. If he gets it going it will be our salvation from this cursed ship."

Sam came close to getting a taste of salt water from all the crew after Bob was ordered to make a clandestine check of all water casks. Valentine had originally told Sam to check the casks, and this done the crew were told that two fifteen-gallon casks lashed up for'ard were empty. When Bob checked them he discovered the port one had two gallons in it. Sam stood accused of siphoning off his own supply.

After three days' effort Bully started the engine. However, Valentine told them the engine used one gallon of petrol per mile and therefore had to be reserved for an emergency. This did not stop all hands using the petrol for cooking, however. Paraffin had run out and unbelievably they were using petrol in the Primus stoves. It just happened to be Sam's luck that a stove exploded while he was using it. His clothes caught fire and he rushed on deck screaming. Bully dowsed him with water while Braun, in a panic, rather rashly threw flour on the flames issuing from the Primus stove. A chain was organised and they put out the blaze with buckets of water.

The mood of the crew blackened considerably, and when Sam announced that he was going to drink the alcohol in the compass Bob threatened to hit him. Bob later wrote: "Had a lot of trouble with him [Sam] during this voyage and it may come to a fight before we make port. I hope so, anyway."

Was Cocos exerting some diabolical magnetic field? After five weeks the schooner and its simmering crew had still not reached Panama, and adverse winds and currents still hindered progress.

Thirty-six days out the the foremast crashed over the side in a cloud of dry rot dust. Bob organised the crew to hack away the rotten mast and dump it over the side, add new rigging to the mainmast and set two jury foresails. By late afternoon they had finished and Valentine rewarded them with a tot of the brandy he had been keeping well hidden.

That same day they managed to attract the attention of a passing steamship, the *Canadian Britisher*. Sam rowed over in a boat with a radiogram requesting a tug. At 1.30 pm the following day they were taken in tow by the United States Navy tug *Ortolan*.

During the *Franklin Barnett's* exasperating voyage, Bob penned the old song his grand-uncle Louis used to sing. The words he used to listen to all those years ago in family parlours had an eerie application to the *Thelma's* voyage and the Black Schooner's deliverance.

"Jonas hated work and toil
He could not his master please
All young Jonas really wanted
Was to live a life of ease.

Weary of the autumn ploughing
Weary of his arduous call
Jonas felt a nudge beside him
'Twas the devil, horns and all.

'Sell to me your soul my Jonas
For a hundred golden pounds
No more work and no more ploughing
Drink your wine and ride to hounds.'

Jonas shook hands with the devil
'Take my soul and have your joy
I'll be termed an English gallant
'Stead of just a farmer's boy.

'Give me now your hundred sovereigns
I'll no more these furrows tread
Let me burst these bonds of toil
You can have me when I'm dead.'

Jonas bought a fine young chestnut
Ordered flagons rich and rare
But where'er he went he noticed
Master devil he was there.

Soon the hundred pounds was fading
Thirty, twenty, ten then nine
Jonas felt the breath of Hades
Every time he drank his wine.

Dark and dread remorse struck Jonas
Wished he had not left his plough
And the devil ever beckoning
Said, 'Why don't you come down now?'

'I have not spent all your money
Can we not a bargain clasp?
Save me from the flames of Hades
And I'll do what e'er you ask.'

'There is only one course open
Give me back what doth remain
You must sail the stormy ocean
Never to come home again.'

Jonas did as he was bidden
Once more with him he shook hands
Thought perhaps he'd pay him one day
With some gold from far-off land.

Sadly to the strand went Jonas
With the devil at his side
'There's the lofty ship you'll sail in
Dropping on the falling tide.'

Then the longboat came for Jonas
Took him from his native shore
Once aboard the bark poor Jonas
Stared in wonder and in awe.

All the crew were hauling, gasping
Heaving on the topsail sheet
And he saw that from their breeches
There protruded cloven feet.

So all you who till the soil
Bend your backs and steer your plough
Or you'll end with wretched Jonas
Writhing in the flames below."

Back in Cristóbal Bob and Bully started to search for the boat that would replace the *Thelma* and carry them to Tahiti, then on round the world. They surveyed a thirty-foot charcoal carrier called the *Adelaide* but they could not afford the £600 asking price. They also looked over a thirty-eight-foot yawl, the *Normandy*, but she was almost a wreck. Although the pair were willing to reconstruct her the owner wanted £200, which Bob considered a joke.

Bob was very reluctant to return to Britain. They had come half way on their adventure and they had a sneaking feeling that somehow it would never be recommenced from home. However, they realised that they would have to go home to earn. The British consul came up with an imaginative proposal to get them a free passage back to Liverpool. A steamship stoker had gone mad in the engine room of an outward-bound vessel; if the brawny young sailors would act as his escort home their fares would be paid. Consequently they shipped aboard the *Orbita*. Bob noted: "Although there is a fine NE breeze and a short, choppy sea it seems as though we are looking out from a pier. So high up out of the water and to us almost imperceptible motion makes it look as though these steamship sailors are merely landsmen adrift."

Bob and Bully's duty included listening to their charge, Joe, believing he was a radio announcer and telling the world about his two companions, President Roosevelt (Bully) and Jack Dempsey (Bob). His declaration that the chief steward was Greta Garbo had the guardians wondering just how insane he was supposed to be! One night he tried to fight the pair and they were ordered by the ship's doctor to frog-march him to his padded cell.

At the end of their voyage Bob concluded his log with an affectionate appreciation of his faithful friend Bully. "From time to time in this journal I have expressed my opinions in what I believe to be honest and frank terms. I hope when he [Bully] reads this diary he will not take any offence at remarks herein, which are merely an expression of my feelings at the time.

"In conclusion—I have enjoyed every day of the past year and I'll go to any part of the world in any sort of ship provided I have got Bully as mate. . . ."

A tattered, faded photograph of Bully with the pig which he and Sinsbury shot on Cocos.
Mrs Sheila Roberts

CHAPTER SEVEN

More Yachting

THE MUD still popped and spat as the receding grey tide deposited the Erith Yacht Club headquarters on the south bank of Erith Rands. The ramshackle boardwalks and slipways were still humped in their crippled way across the back of the marsh but other things had changed.

A new member twice Bob's age had arrived at the Club and was talking big. The fit, tanned, wiry little man had plans that were making ripples on Bob's pond. Ernie Sinclair, a well-read, well-educated retired schoolmaster, reminded Bob of his father with his academic outlook on matters marine. With an acid and cynical wit used unsparingly on those less articulate than himself, Ernie soon made enemies. Bully dropped out of the Erith scene and found a job with a small engineering firm.

Bob, desperate to get away again, suffered the pompous sophistication of Ernie's bearing and looked for his good points. One of them was the fact that the prestigious Little Ship Club was found by Ernie and two companions to be rather shy of the rude and rollicky ribaldry of which they were fond.

Instead, Ernie and his pals founded their own club, the Narrow Seas Club. They also resented the fact that motorboat owners were beginning to proliferate in the Little Ship Club. To check such "rot" taking hold potential members of the Narrow Seas Club had to be sponsored by at least five members. They had a "skipper" rather than a commodore, and the first to hold the title was Ernie. Their constitution was a written one and euphemistically simple: "To provide facilities for social intercourse among men interested in the handling of small craft." Its splinter-group style made it a bedouin club, travelling from one existing clubhouse to a receptive pub for its meetings. Bob joined in 1935, three years after it was founded.

Ernie Sinclair was planning a deep-sea cruise and he was aiming westwards across the Atlantic. The boat he had in mind was the fifty-seven-foot Ramsgate trawler *Quartette*. Ernie's seniority and solvency meant that the young and penniless Bob soon realised his position on board would be as number two. Bob and Ernie went down to Ramsgate in October, 1934, and bought the *Quartette* between them for £110. Bob felt guilty to be taking the vessel out of trade and into pleasure sailing, for she was the last vessel to fish out of Ramsgate under sail alone, an historical depletion that Bob would one day experience himself.

They sailed her round to Whitstable to fit out, and the last remaining crew

John Bell preparing dinner while the *Quartette* steers herself on a tiller line.   *Mrs Sheila Trefusis*

member, Harry Solly, went with them. Bob was absorbed listening to the old man tell of the days when seven men went fishing in her. He tried to forget, and hoped Harry had not heard, Ernie's order as they left Ramsgate harbour. When they were about to take in the mooring lines as the stern and bow lines were cast off, Ernie gave the order, "Undo it."

The *Quartette* was to have her bottom refastened and metal sheathing tacked on. The rest of the work required, such as making the standing and running rigging, Bob was prepared to do himself. While the work on her hull was under way Bob cycled to London to earn money from other rigging jobs on yachts. When he eventually arrived back at Whitstable, on his bicycle to save on fares, he was staggered to find the *Quartette* almost ready for sea.

Bob had expected to share a bill of £150 for the hull work. Now he faced a bill of £537. He had earned £75 for his rigging work in London and fretted over the huge bill. Ernie brushed aside his fears, accepted only £50 of Bob's £75 and assured him the rest did not matter. He would be happy with some deep water cruising.

Bob was not happy feeling compromised: "I now owe him £218 approx. and have no real means of paying it off. It will always be a weight on my mind. Whatever he says I feel morally bound to pay it off or else offer to surrender my interest in the vessel."

Bob and Ernie advertised in a yachting magazine for two extra hands to join them and share expenses. They selected two men, John Bell from West Mersea in Essex and Henry Trefusis from Falmouth. They agreed to sail to Mersea to pick up John and all his gear. As they left the East Swale with a steady southerly wind Bob, for the second time, had doubts about sailing with Ernie. Bob was aloft changing the lead of a halyard when he felt the heavy old trawler shudder. Ernie had sailed inside the buoys marking the Spaniard, a drying knoll of sand in the approaches to the West Swale. The *Quartette* had run right on to the highest part, and as the ebb tide swirled away she began to lay over.

The following day, sailing into Mersea, Ernie again put her ashore, this time on the Nass sand. "I always regarded Ernie as the complete seaman," wrote Bob, "but I find that in many things he is very much an amateur yachtsman. As a skipper his orders are neither definite nor convincing." In Mersea Quarters Bob swallowed hard as Ernie ordered him to "tie on" the dinghy instead of using the seamanlike phrase "make it fast". Bob continued "Perhaps my early seafaring days spoiled me for understanding his ways, for I was steeped in ritual and tradition. He even refers to the deck as 'upstairs'! I am not prepared to say that such things make him any the poorer seaman in practice but they coincide with the unfortunate fact that I have already begun to lose confidence in him. His ways are not the ways of a sailor; neither does his talk savour of the sea."

John Bell shipped aboard, a "lanky, delicate, nervous and rather public schoolish" hand, Bob noted. Bob also recognised a quiet calm about him not dissimilar from that which existed in Bully. Bully was contentedly out of it all but once more helped Bob out by making up some fittings for the *Quartette* at cost price.

Henry Trefusis on board *Quartette*.
Mrs Sheila Trefusis

The *Quartette* completed her fitting out and victualling in the East India Dock. Ernie ordered a tow from Erith, after the crew had spent a weekend there at the Yacht Club, which cost thirty shillings (£1.50). Bob, who was not in command, was powerless to suggest that they sail to the dock and thus save adding to the relentlessly lengthening bill. The Antarctic exploration ship *Discovery* lay next to them in the dock and the *Quartette* gained a ship's cat from a litter reared by the ancient vessel's caretaker. They christened her *Disco*.

Henry Trefusis, an Oxford graduate, joined the ship at Falmouth. Both he and John were paying crew. Bob, as mate, started to keep the ship's log but after Ernie interfered, with his indomitable claims to be captain, Bob handed over the log completely to him. Bob wrote: "Sinclair has butted in and messed up my system. Now it's going to look more like a landsman's diary judging from his 'ditto' winds etc."

With such a well-educated crew aboard, John started an off-watch game to pass the time. Called the *Literary Rag-Bag*, it was a notebook left on the saloon table for those who felt like it to make their mark in verse. One of the first verses penned was by Henry, who had also begun to notice Ernie's dubious seamanship. He scrawled the lines in his private log as he worked on the first draft:

> "The *Quartette's* Skipper doesn't know a thing about log-keeping,
> You can tell from the entries in it dumped;
> Such as 'Porpoises around us gave a fine display of leaping' and 'a fish like a
> big plaice jumped'.
> 'Turned inwards' and 'turned outwards' and 'went on other tack'.
> What a lousy way of saying 'put about'!
> He even tells us things we seek are 'upstairs at the back'.
> These phrases we can gladly do without.
> From all this you may gather we are fed up with our wee man.
> For the bounder is as useless as can be,
> If the fellow cannot think, act, talk, or write things like a seaman
> Why the devil does the blighter go to sea?"

It was never entered in the *Rag-Bag*.

Six days out from Falmouth the peak halyards chafed through. Bob cursed the Whitstable yard. He had wanted to reeve the halyards himself not just to save money but also because he believed the yard would rig out the *Quartette* like a trawler rather than for long, rolling swells where chafe had to be endured.

The precarious job of climbing out along the gaff to reeve a new one was left to Bob. Forty-seven years later, John Bell recalled Bob's climb:

"One event I shall always remember was the parting of the main peak halyard. The gaff was as long as the boom and a beastly heavy spar it was, and high peaked. The main gaff was left supported by the topsail sheet, which looked woefully inadequate for the job. Bob decided it was unsafe to start the topsail sheet or halyard or the main throat halyard and crawled out along the

Disco the cat, who died at sea and was given a sailor's burial off the mouth of the Amazon.

Mrs Sheila Trefusis

gaff with a new peak halyard. None of the others of us could have done it. It required great strength and nerve and we were glad when he had made it safe aloft and come down again."

Henry wrote in his own log; "Spectacular acrobatics on the part of the mate who got the parts seized together and we were able to carry on without lowering the mainsail."

Bob's own spartan entry simply reads: "Peak halyard parted 1 pm. Repaired same temporarily but shall be unable to lower mainsail."

Four days later the weather was suitable for lowering the mainsail to reeve a new halyard and this time Bob decided to allow the two passengers to show their mettle. "Made our amateurs go aloft and help with the work there but they were not much use. John got a bit scared and came down on deck in very short time. Henry kept singing out 'aye-aye' in seamanlike fashion but at the same time let go the wrong rope and allowed the halyard to unreeve again. Decided that my previous convictions were correct. If a job has to be done aboard here it is simpler in the end to do it myself and not ask for any help at all."

At Madeira Bob's pent up frustration almost boiled over. Ernie used the excuse of the main sheet block, which needed tending, to declare that he did not think much of the mate's attitude. There were some strong words but the pair reached an accord without violence. As Bob put it: "We do not want to break up the cruise here in Madeira and be the joke of all the people who wished us well in England a few weeks ago. Like most little men I think he has a hot temper."

One night in Las Palmas Bob was the last person to turn in when he noticed Disco disappear over the side. The thought of losing the one capable "hand" aboard the *Quartette* spurred Bob into calling the rest of them on deck. He and Ernie actually jumped over the side! The cat was eventually brought back aboard. The bedraggled object, shivering pathetically, had no sympathy from John. He had already experienced Bob's wrath over "mistreating" the animal.

John wrote: "Bob became absurdly fond of the black kitten he brought from the *Discovery*. When the kitten grew into a fine strong cat it exercised itself by tearing from one end of the ship to the other; when doing this below deck one evening it included in its exercise track the length of my body. After about a dozen passages over me I got fed up and struck at it. Bob was furious. It was not on account of anything done to him. That was what he was like."

John's idea of the *Literary Rag-Bag* was shrewd. It proved invaluable as a safety valve. The nightwatchman coming down off duty could release his fury in a few lines of verse. Then, while he was turned in, the next man up could read it alone, chuckle, add his own view and forget about it. At its best the *Rag-Bag* literally spliced relations together again.

"As I was lying in my bed
The mate he thumped me on the head
He said turn out and come on deck
Or you will get it in the neck"   *Henry*

"I came on deck with my eyes bunged up
and asked the mate if I could sup
He said: 'No damn you, do your stuff
I've been on deck here long enough'"   *Bob*

"I took the helm and soon alack
I found I'd got her flat aback
The mate came roaring from below
And told me plainly where to go"   *Henry*

"The boom-guy parted, bang she went
The bowsprit whipped and the mainmast bent
The mainsail split and the gaff came down
I felt that I should like to drown"   *Bob*

Ernie never made an entry.

When the north-east trade winds died away and left the *Quartette* in the doldrums Bob became interested in another pastime which in later life became his hallmark: "Am learning to play Henry's accordion. I find it easier than I expected. Repertoire so far includes 'Bobby Shaftoe', 'Early in the Morning', 'Drink to me Only', and 'Alous a Messina'. Will buy one for myself if I attain any degree of proficiency."

As they drifted along, large rainbow-coloured translucent jellyfish pulsated slowly round the ship. Another game was invented called "Nelson's gob" in which the competitor had to try and get a whole Portuguese man-of-war in a bucket.

The conflict between Bob and Ernie was never very far away. Henry and John found Ernie difficult to get along with as well but really their argument was as partisans. They sided with the stronger man.

John Bell aboard the *Quartette* in 1935.
Mrs Sheila Trefusis

Ernie showed his isolation in deliberately petty ways. He would wash up the knives and forks after they had already been cleaned and put away by one of the others. He scraped the primus gimbals, polished the bottom of the kettle, even scraped scrapers after use! These fits of pique became known as Annie Palavers. Among the others Ernie was rechristened "Annie".

Two days out of São Tomé, an island off the West Coast of Africa, Ernie started using the fresh water to wash the dishes. "I made a long and diplomatic speech to the old man on the value of drinking water," wrote Bob. "He was completely agreeable and I thought I had hit on the head his scheme of using the water for washing up and bathing. No bloody fear. Half an hour after he drew off two gallons of drinking water to wash up with. John and Henry seem quite indignant about it. He certainly is a bloody fool. Probably at 60 his savvy is not so good as it was. Henry emphatically asserts that the old chap is 'gaga' as he calls it."

John, sensing the increasing darkness of the mood between Bob and Ernie, put a warning in the *Rag-Bag*:

> "O men may sing and dance at sea
> And some to muse are able.
> But perish the man who writes bad verse
> and leaves it on the table."

37

CHAPTER EIGHT

Log of Despair

DEEP-SEA voyaging with crew who were paying for their time aboard was no way to run a ship, Bob decided. A ship's company obeyed orders and shrugged off rough remarks because that was their job. Passengers on a ship expected top service and safe passage as well as courtesy from the crew because they were paying for it. On a vessel such as the *Quartette* the crew were paying passengers and Bob felt his position as mate was undermined by this status of the crew.

He noted: "Henry is getting a bit irksome to us all lately. He thinks we ought to gybe, lay a different course, set a different sail—ought to do this, ought to do that etc etc. To prevent any quarrelling I have to endure this in silence principally because H is paying £8.10.0 (£8.50) a month for the honour of sailing in this ship."

Later, when Bob ordered Henry to alter course by half a point, Henry retorted, "Damned ridiculous," probably with some justification! Bob was furious. "Felt very much like punching him on the nose. I'm dead scared that one day at sea I'll get so bloody fed up with him and the Old Man that I'll hit somebody. Wouldn't I like to get these two in my watch in a trading schooner! Gee, I'd give 'em hell and a sore ass."

During a particularly dirty night while Ernie and Henry were on watch they had to get the topsail off her. According to Bob it was a hash job. "Judging by the excitement, stamping and shouting one would have thought they were tacking a full-rigged ship. According to Henry, Ern did not know the halyard from the sheet or tack from jackstay. I can quite believe this. Result was they got the sail all round their necks and Joe Soap had to turn out and rescue them.

"Each bloke then came up to me and confided that the other was no bloody good.

"Ern says he wants to learn something about that topsail. Having been skipper for six months it has just dawned on him that he does not know either

Bob Roberts with bananas aboard the *Quartette*.
Mrs Sheila Trefusis

how to set it or how to take it in." It was mainly Ernie of whom Bob despaired. The *Quartette* nearly missed Ascension Island altogether. Bob discovered Ernie had applied the variation the wrong way for three days.

Henry retreated into his rhymes. He realised Bob was the superior seaman. Poor Henry had planned a season's racing. Throughout his logbook were scattered the dates for the Channel Race, St Malo Race, Fastnet, Plymouth–Belle Isle Race, among others. If only he had gone ahead with his original plans.

He scribbled in the *Rag-Bag*:

> "Now hark while I tell
> Of our mate, who's the hell
>   of a he-man
>
> He's a bit of all right
> The two ends and the bight
>   of a sea-man."

Bob made efforts to cheer Henry and John. He wrote out his charges for hair-cutting, a duty he had adopted.

"Quartette Barbery.

Hair cut	1 bot. beer.
Shampoo	1 glass whisky (no water).
Beard trim	½ hour's helm.
Shave	1 cigar.
Eyebrows plucked	free."

Left: The *Quartette* in harbour.
Mrs Sheila Trefusis

Opposite: A view of the *Quartette's* deck; the bowsprit is run in.
Mrs Sheila Trefusis

And the following ditty in the *Rag-Bag*:

> "Nein vint por days
> Ein glassy swell
> Nor est monsoon
> Est bloody hell
>
> Ein breezen come
> El mate lots cheer
> Because now
> El schipper steer.
>
> A Rio go
> We makum soon
> Los letters vill
> Be bueno boon.
>
> El Mato."

Henry got the taste for some of the same:

> "Flat calm in the South Atlantic
> Beneath a scorching sun
> The crew are driven frantic
> By our negligible run
> The deck is hot as Hades,
> The sun strikes through your hat,
> The cat lies where the shade is
> Though there is not much of that!

Sinclair on the *Quartette's* deck.
Mrs Sheila Trefusis

Flat calm in the South Atlantic
Beneath a waving moon
The swell has grown gigantic,
We've logged four miles since noon.
Your watch on deck is boring,
You cannot hope to steer,
The watch below are snoring,
Two hours seems like a year!"

They played deck cricket in the calms, using a petrol can for the wicket, hatch batten as a bat and rotten limes for balls.

Ernie excelled himself as Bob was shaking a reef out of the mizzen. As Bob trimmed out the clew of the sail with the reefing tackle, Ernie popped up from the galley with two dishcloths and clipped them with pegs on the very tackle Bob was hauling, then disappeared below again!

When they reached Rio de Janeiro John allowed himself one weekend's boozing with his old shipmates before leaving for home in a steamer. He told Bob before he left that he could stand Ernie no longer.

Henry wrote another rhyme which he did not enter in the *Rag-Bag*:

"Now when we sailed from Rio
Quartette became a trio
For one wise man had booked his passage home.
And as soon as I can do it
Quartette will be a duet,
For I have satisfied my wish to roam."

The voyage dragged on. After a long period of heavy weather Bob made a list of repairs he had carried out. He had spliced the main peak vang and the vang, restitched the main peak cringle, and refastened the mizzen sheet cleat after it had broken off. He had also fixed the for'ard pin rail which had been carried away, and later spliced the mizzen peak halyard and the topsail downhaul. "All these things I have had to repair and patch up myself. H helps as much as he can but Sinclair is quite incapable of being the slightest use. In any case he hardly ever notices anything that goes wrong on deck. He is about as observant as a blind owl.

"I'll be glad to get shot of him even if I lose my share in the boat. I'd rather sail with some old woman for a skipper. What a fraud he has been to live on a false reputation for so many years."

Bob kept his spirits up by continual practice on the accordion. *Disco* was weighted and dropped overboard after expiring from a crippling disease. Bob poignantly noted his last berth: "Lat 2 degrees North Long 44 degrees 50 minutes west off the mouth of the Amazon."

On arrival in Port of Spain, Trinidad, Henry paid £18 for his passage home in a Fyffe ship. Ernie did not even wish him goodbye. Henry took with him Bob's last entry for the *Literary Rag-Bag*, which he also took away with him:

> "Wrap him [Ernie] up in his red bathing costume
> and throw the   over the side.
> We'll say that we lost him at mid-night.
> And no one will know that we lied."

Bob's flagging spirits now took a dive. He told Ernie what he thought of him and that his disagreeableness had been the blight of the cruise, scaring away the crew and making the *Quartette* an unwelcome ship in port.

Ernie kept quiet, but the pair surprisingly decided to sail back to England together if they could not sell the ship. This thought depressed Bob and he had to dream up a future to get him through it. He decided a flat-bottomed craft such as a barge would be a good prospect for trading in some of the shallower areas of the Caribbean and he hoped Bully would sail a barge to the West Indies with him, to run oil between Trinidad and British Guiana. Bob need not have worried. The *Quartette* was sold to a fishing company, Messrs Canning, Boyce and Scott, for £300, and was taken to Barbados to have an ice tank fitted. Bob and Ernie got rooms ashore in Rosolin Street for six dollars a month each.

For a while Bob considered the possibility of the mate's job on the schooner *Frances W. Smith* of Bridgetown, Barbados. She was carrying case oil, rice, sugar, lumber and cocoa between Trinidad, Demerara and Barbados. In the end he decided that, more than anything, he wanted his own command and returned home in a Dutch ship as a third class passenger paying £16.

Bob's days of blue-water wandering were over.

Two months later Bob delivered his final blow to a bitter voyage. The following appeared under his name in *Yachting Monthly* dated 1st May, 1936:

"The fact that a man has crossed the Atlantic or made some daring passages in small boats does not prove that he is a good seaman. Most small boat passages of any great duration are achieved by blissful ignorance and the Grace of God.

"It seems that the less a man knows about the sea the more likely he is to succeed in a stunt cruise. For that is what most small boat voyages are, no matter what pose the participants assume."

Stories reached the Erith Yacht Club of a further yacht voyage by Ernie Sinclair, to Hawaii.

Meanwhile Bully had agreed to sail with Bob and the search was on for a ship. Bob Roberts was master once again.

Ernie Sinclair at *Quartette's* helm and Bob Roberts during the voyage.

CHAPTER NINE

Into Trade

BENEATH the mauve-blue slopes of Sugar Loaf Mountain lies the harbour of Wicklow in Ireland. In 1936, Bob and Bully were hard at work aboard an old topsail schooner called the *B.I.* Although it was Bob's £160 that paid for her it is Bully's name on the Bill of Sale. It was a crafty move to cut out the agent's fee. Bob made all the inquiries and found out what sum would be acceptable, then sent Bully along to the owner with an "independent" offer.

Their arrival in Wicklow had been preceded by a journey to the little village of Mistley in Essex where they had gone to search for a barge. Mistley was the kingdom of the Horlock barging family. If they had anything for sale it was only because there was no further use for it. After a couple of nights at *The Thorn* pub Bob and Bully abandoned their search and turned instead to what was then called the Irish Free State.

Bob had been promised freights from the London and Rochester Trading Company (now called Crescent Shipping) to ports down-Channel. Bully was mate on a share basis.

Bob loved his new command. He wrote to his old friend Lewis: "She is a lovely old vessel capable of carrying 180 tons on a handy draught of 10ft 6in." The *B.I.* was eighty-seven feet long, built of teak and oak and sixty years old; she had been built at Shoreham as the *Sarah Ann* in 1874. Bob planned to employ two hands to sail her. Meanwhile he employed local lads to tar and caulk the hull and was impressed by their hard work. One lad worked all day and all night "with only a cup of tea and a piece of bread inside him".

The lad, Jim Kehoe, had only one ambition—to be a labourer in England. Bob wrote to Lewis asking him to help find the boy a job. "I can now quite understand why you have Irish labourers. They certainly do put some guts into the job. Wages are very low and the cost of living atrociously high. Everyone seems terribly poor and yet the steady supply of large broods of children passes my comprehension. Scores of kids scamper about in the mud, barefoot along with the chickens, dogs, pigs, etc—all mixed up together and all indescribably dirty and ill-fed looking."

They eventually got the old schooner loaded with loam and gravel for Falmouth but the south-westerly gale they encountered off Wexford Bay opened her up badly and she started to sink. As Bully pumped continuously Bob sailed for the River Suir, which he skilfully found in the dark without proper charts.

The following day the pair beached her at a place called Passage East. The local customs officer had contacted the Board of Trade and reported the *B.I.*'s arrival "in distress". As a result, an official surveyor was sent down to inspect the ship. He insisted on prohibitively expensive repairs and refused to pass her as seaworthy unless the work was carried out by local shipwrights rather than the crew.

"We were trespassing," explained Bully. "We were trying to get in on their local trade so it was a conspiracy to prevent us taking their work."

They had not got the money to match the repairs required. The *B.I.* was sold at an auction to the highest bidder.

The old schooner continued to cause unrest in the otherwise peaceful Suir river. She was towed a few miles further up the river to the village of Cheekpoint. Here her owner employed a retired master, Captain Burns, to act as a resident watchman.

His troubles inspired a poem by a local resident called Bill Dwyer. The following excerpt chronicles the "curse" of the *B.I.* suffered by Bob's successor:

> "With an ugly list on her starboard bow
> With her mainsails gone and boom
> Now her guardian angel was Capt Burns
> With Darkie as nom de plume
> She was auctioned as scrap and a Tramore man
> Her trapping and all did buy
> He promised the Capt 10 shillings a week
> To watch o'er the schooner B.I.
>
> When the captain slept one stormy night
> Some fellows came in a boat
> Went aboard the schooner and took some rope
> They needed to tether a goat
> When the captain found his loss next day
> He raised a terrible cry
> For he did not know what the owner would say
> To the theft on the schooner B.I.
>
> When the owner came and heard the news
> A wrathful man was he
> He told the captain he was no use
> He knew nothing of land or sea
>
> Now Capt. Burns was an honest man
> He resented the owner's remarks
> He said since I took charge of your hulk
> I've been working from dawn till dark
> I've welts on my feet from tramping her decks
> Now pay me my wages my boy
> And I bid you farewell you may go to hell
> Yourself and the schooner B.I.

The remains of the *B.I.* are still being picked over more than fifty years on. Alf Doherty, whose waterside home looks over the schooner's bones, said: "I got a lot of firewood from her. She'll keep me warm for many a winter." He has also salvaged her anchors, painted them white and decorated his front garden with them.

When Bob left the *B.I.* to her fate, it would be thirty years before he owned a ship again.

The luckless sailors returned to England. Bully went off looking for work as an engineer while Bob got his first job aboard a barge as mate of the *Audrey*. A

The schooner *B.I.* in Wicklow harbour in 1936. *Mrs Sheila Roberts*

The barge *Oceanic*, in which Bob Roberts was mate for a short time. She is seen here with a deck cargo off Southend Pier.   *Tony Farnham collection*

year in her and he was aching to get into larger barges, coasting work and extra pay. He worked for a short time aboard the big steel barge *Oceanic*. His first permanent berth was aboard Alfred Sully's *Oxygen* as mate with a man who became his mentor, Percy Quantrill, of Pin Mill in Suffolk.

Percy was a kind, intelligent skipper who sang hymns out loud in the face of adversity. Bob liked and respected him and stayed mate with him for two years, trading mainly between London and Ipswich. They once took a freight of barley to Snape maltings, which was where Percy finally fell out with his employers after a series of disagreements. Bob and he parted company but Bob never forgot the man who once commented, as they tried to get ashore at Walton-on-Naze, trudging backwards and forwards between the backwaters. "It's like being in Venice without any money."

The new skipper of the *Oxygen* arrived and with Bob sailed back to Sittingbourne, where Bob's first barge awaited him.

The *Hambrook*, or *Hambone* as they called her, was built at Sittingbourne in 1883. Just a little barge, forty-eight tons, she nevertheless was the beginning of Bob's long career as master of sailing barges. He returned to his old haunts at Erith to find a mate and announced in the bar of the Yacht Club that he was looking for a hand.

Harry Bottreill had been a clerk at Chappells, the music publishers of Bond Street, for twelve years. A safe if rather dull job. Something about Bob excited his sense of adventure. Harry and his two brothers had been rebuilding an eighteen-foot yacht among the other old hulks of Erith marshes. Now, out of the blue, was the chance of turning weekend adventures into the real thing.

Harry said: "Bob came in and said, 'I'm looking for a mate'. And for some unknown reason I didn't think about it. I just said, 'Will I do?'"

Bob asked him if he could cook eggs and bacon and tie a bowline, and remained unperturbed on learning that he could not scull a boat very well. Bob told Harry to sign on the following day at Sittingbourne at 8 am, to which Harry replied, "I've got to give notice. Make it Tuesday."

Harry said: "My brothers sat there with their mouths open. However, I'd done it, and that was that."

One of the first freights was maize to Battlesbridge on the River Crouch. At Hullbridge they picked up a floating log connected to a length of chain. With the

Bob Roberts' mentor, Percy Quantrill, aboard the barge *Ena* in Yarmouth harbour. In the background can be seen a number of steam herring drifters.   *Mrs May Quantrill*

anchor down and the chain made fast aft the barge could not swing athwart the river. Here they waited for the huffler-pilot to take them up to the mill. They were joined by another barge, the *Pride of Ipswich*, skippered by Rodney White. The *Hambrook* was first up to the mill. That night it blew a gale of wind. The next morning Rodney stepped on board with tears in his eyes and the incredible tale that his barge had sunk. She had sat on a pile of old chain used to anchor the log and this had pushed right through her bottom.

As soon as the *Hambrook* had unloaded, Bob was ordered by Sully's, who had a half share in the *Pride* along with the skipper, to load her spoilt cargo of maize. Harry said: "We had to use picks and shovels to get it out because it had swelled so much and pushed the planking of the barge apart. It was slimy and very hot. We took it up the London River to the Desiccated Grain Company. The gas from

Bob Roberts' first command, the little *Hambrook*, on the mud off Leigh-on-Sea in 1933.
Tony Farnham collection

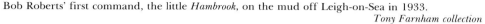

Cambria, on left, and *Royalty* being towed into Yarmouth by the paddle tug *United Service*, a photograph taken by Clifford Temple in the nineteen-thirties.   *Tony Farnham collection*

the stuff put out the cabin lamps and during the voyage we left most of the hatches off. We looked like a motorship with all the steam coming off it."

Bob swore blind the spoilt maize went into the production of corn flakes.

The *Hambrook* was a blunt-ended old thing and not particularly swift. They started missing freights and Bob went to see Mr Burley, the owner, to ask him for a faster barge. He got it and took Harry with him into the *Northdown*. She had made a name for herself racing, making the pair very proud to be shipping aboard her. Nevertheless still they were lumbered with short, poorly-paid freights of coal from London to Sittingbourne.

Eventually they broke free of the river trade and fixed the barge with 150 tons of oil cake used for cattle feed from the Millwall Docks to Great Yarmouth.

Sailing out of the Thames they had the wind on the quarter when a change of course meant a gybe was necessary. As the gear swung over, the sprit collapsed on deck with a terrific crash. Harry saw that the sprit was absolutely rotten. "Bob picked up great chunks of putty, some of it two feet long, four inches wide and two inches thick. The whole thing had been patched up. Burley had no right to send anyone away to sea with a thing like that. The chaps at the yard had patched this damned thing up, filled up all the holes, then painted nicely over it."

This happened off Shoeburyness in Essex. Bob discussed his plans with Harry and asked his opinion before deciding to make a jury rig of the gear and

51

sail on to Yarmouth. As they approached Yarmouth the steam paddle tug *United Service* came out and the skipper, Harry Wright, yelled, "Going to make a job of it Bob?" Bob knew the man wanted him to declare he was a wreck in order that he could claim salvage. Bob told him where to go, saying only that he was prepared to pay double the towage rates. The tug returned to Yarmouth and left them at the mercy of the weather; all night they tended their crippled barge.

Next morning the charade was repeated, with the tug coming out to them and returning at Bob's refusal to admit he was a marine casualty. Eventually the skipper of the tug agreed to double towage rates and took them in.

Harry said: "We were up all night watching the weather very carefully, because if it had come on shore we wouldn't have stood a chance. Not a nice position, trying to hold that bloody stump of a sprit in position in November time. But it was unfortunate because it didn't do Harry Wright any good. His name was mud for a bit and that was very sad because the old fellow had taken a lot of chances when it came to rescuing barges." Mr Wright was due to retire and, so the story went, was hoping for a fat pay-off from the salvage of the limping *Northdown*, but he had not reckoned on Bob Roberts.

Yarmouth was built on a sandbank which formed across the mouth of a great estuary a thousand years ago. Its precarious topography earned Yarmouth the reputation of being the worst harbour on the east coast for bargemen to enter. Not even that would have forced Bob to give up. Neither jury rig nor a blackmailing tug skipper could scare him.

"He was a go-getter," stated Harry. "There was no question about it. He didn't discuss the voyage under jury rig. He didn't consider it to be an accomplishment. It was part of the job and he took it that way. I never heard him boast about this. He didn't show off, nor was he after a reputation. He didn't care what the others did about the weather or anything else, and rightly so."

Bob was watched by other bargemen and sometimes cursed by them as well. For his stoic way of passage-making landed perhaps more wary, nervous or simply lazy bargemen in hot water with their employers. No better example of this could be had than the trip back up made by the *Northdown* after she had been fitted with a new sprit at Yarmouth. The same southerly wind which blew them there had also been holding up barges already lying at Yarmouth. There were many gathered waiting for a shift of wind. When it eventually came it was blowing hard from the south-west. For a few hours one day the wind westered and Bob was off. He had a fast barge and a young and fit mate, and he reckoned if he could weather Orfordness before the wind backed he could make a passage.

All the other crews sat on their hatches watching the *Northdown* tow out of the harbour.

Harry explained their feelings: "If we got to London and they didn't, immediately the owners would be on to them and say, 'What's the matter with you? What are you lying there for? Why don't you get on with it? If the

Northdown can do it then you can.' This was the reason for the disaster during the gale. I'm sure of that. They felt that if they didn't go and we got through then they would be in for it. The point I want to make about Bob here is that he wasn't vicious. It was a question of getting on with the job, doing it well and not wasting any damned time." They did not waste any time. They managed to reach Harwich and safety as the wind backed to the south-west and blew a gale.

Meanwhile, the other barges came out. The skippers had changed their minds, but the time they had wasted proved to be disastrous. Lifeboats from Yarmouth, Lowestoft, Southwold and Aldeburgh were launched to assist or rescue crews from seven barges, two of which drove right across the North Sea and piled up on the Dutch coast.

When the *Northdown* eventually arrived back in London Mr Burley was waiting to see Bob and Harry. He handed them a £5 note each for saving the barge and to their astonishment told them she had not been insured! Like it or not, Bob now had a reputation.

He had broken in to barging. Bob was aware of the doubts other bargemen had about him. He was from the blue waters and deep rivers of the West Country. He had a name for being a schoonerman which he did not discourage, although his experience in those craft had been limited. Sail power had died earlier in Devon and Cornwall than it had in the great delta of shoal waters which formed the Thames Estuary. The survival of sail in the Thames Estuary was due to one of the most efficient rigs ever designed, the spritsail. Bob wanted to be accepted among the barging fraternity. His father had not been a bargeman, his family were not from Kent or Essex but he played on his mother's roots in Kessingland, Suffolk. It was Suffolk that he studied. It was Suffolk realities and myths he listened to and passed on. Suffolk where he went to live.

Wary of being criticised, Bob was still choosing crew from yacht clubs, or rather from one yacht club in particular. He did not want to risk a bargeman as

Bob Roberts in the nineteen-forties.
Mrs Sheila Roberts

mate, not at first, not until he had been accepted. Conversely he did not want the bargemen to know his mates were yachtsmen. While Harry, a thirty year old who had chucked in a life of office work to sail with Bob, was learning the ropes Bob told him to keep his mouth closed in the bargemen's pubs. To remind Harry he was to consider himself a bargeman, not a yachtsman, Bob made disparaging remarks about "amateur" sailors".

"A really smart-looking yacht came by once," recounted Harry. "He wasn't in our road but came deliberately close and shouted 'good morning'. He and his wife were in this boat. He had a nice new mainsail. Bob just grunted. Then the chap said it was a nice breeze for stretching his new sail. Bob said, 'You what? Looks like a dust cloth to me.' He always expressed a profound contempt for yachtsmen. When we joined the Narrow Seas Club people listened to what Bob had to say but he always had this attitude, you know, you're apprentices, as it were."

Bob approached Burley and asked him if he would sell the *Northdown* to him. Burley wanted £1,000, which Bob could not raise.

The last freight they carried in her was oil cake, bran and middlings from London to Newport, Isle of Wight. On the homeward run Bob fell ill as they rounded the North Foreland. He had a searing pain in his abdomen. Harry took the barge all the way up the River Medway although Bob crept up the companionway occasionally to see that all was well.

At Chatham Harry sailed her close to a battleship. He hailed her crew, many of whom were hanging over the sides painting. They struck up a chorus of *Red Sails in the Sunset* as the *Northdown* approached, but stopped when Harry bellowed out, asking if they had a doctor aboard. Harry anchored and let go the topsail as Bob lay in agony on his bunk. A naval launch arrived and Bob was taken to Chatham Cottage Hospital.

The amount of form-filling that faced Bob in his stricken state made him ask for an old friend from Erith Yacht Club, "Doc" Harris. He arrived and took Bob away to London, where he diagnosed kidney stones. When Bob next met Harry he told him, to Harry's amusement, that he could drink as much as he liked, as long as it was water and not beer.

While Bob was recovering he received a telegram from the biggest coasting company with the best barges. Mr Bill Everard had heard about the young man who made passages at all costs, whether through gales or under jury rigs and even from his bunk! He was the sort of man who earned the company money. The sort of man to inspire less efficient members of the workforce.

On 24th April, 1939, Bob and Harry shipped aboard the last boomie barge, the *Martinet*, under the "bob" of F. T. Everard and Sons. The boomies were generally similar in construction to the spritsail barges, but instead of having a sprit their mainsail had a conventional gaff and boom, and the sail was lowered when not in use instead of being brailed up, as in the sprittie.

CHAPTER TEN

Martinet

BROWN clouds of rust billowed up in the still air as the huge manacles of old anchor chain snaked down the slipway of George and Thomas Smith's shipyard at Rye. The *Martinet* dragged the bridles of chain from her bows as she was launched, to stop the counter stern at the end of her ninety-five-foot length digging unceremoniously into the mud banks of the deep but narrow River Rother on the opposite side.

As her huge clipper bow curved over the heads of the shipwrights there was a strangely subdued atmosphere, unnatural at a launching, which was normally an excuse for great merriment. It was 1912 and the men who had built the last of the great coasting ketches drank their tots in silence. Up in the churchyard lay a freshly dug grave, the cause of their sobriety.

Rye is a superstitious town. The old sailors still take very seriously the threat of the "Bexhill donkey" as the dreaded rabbit is called. It is well known that rabbits are considered unlucky by seamen, but nowhere is the innocent furry creature more loathed than in Rye. Fishermen working the old sailing smacks refused to put to sea if they as much as laid eyes on one.

When a German luxury liner, the *Elbe*, sank in the North Sea after a collision in 1895, the local men said she must have had rabbits in her bilge. Old Harry Boreham's father was on his way out of the Rother in his smack early one morning when he spotted a corpse high up on the tideline, as the ebb was coming away. He brought up and went ashore, thinking he had found the "Lady of the *Elbe*"; the German government had offered a reward of £50 for every body found. The passengers had been wealthy industrialists and their families were sparing no expense to give them a proper burial.

It was unlikely Harry's father could earn that sort of money in six months, therefore he was very excited when he turned over the corpse to find she had flaxen hair, was very colourfully dressed, had "gold" rings on her fingers and was clutching three coins. He sent his mate back to town to get the police. Alas, by the time they had arrived the "gold" rings had turned brown. As Harry said: "They were all millionaires on that ship and Dad saw the rings and thought he had made it. But they were brass." Subsequent inquiries identified the barmaid of the nearby *Ferry Boat Inn*. She had apparently supplemented her income by entertaining visiting sailors after hours. Locals concluded that she had complained to her client that the three ha'pence she had been found clutching was insufficient reimbursement for her time and that the client had disagreed and tossed her in the river after first knocking her over the head.

It was the fact she kept a rabbit's foot that appalled the Rye men. For them that could never be lucky. Her ghost is said to haunt the *Ferry Boat Inn* to this day.

Into this ancient town inhabited by apprehensive and cautious sailors was born the *Martinet*.

Harry Boreham, who proudly keeps his shipwright's adze in a black box beneath the bed in the old folks' home where he now lives, still remembers the *Martinet*. "She was a smart ship, accordingly there wasn't nothing like her. 'Til she took that shipwright." Although Harry worked five years on the G. and T. Smith shipyard, he was not there when the *Martinet* was built, but such was her reputation that he knew all about her. Even the fishermen believed she would be an unlucky ship, having killed a shipwright during her construction.

Henry Parsons, who sailed on the trawler *Alfred Colebrook*, said: "He was a big man, about twenty-five years old. He liked beer and women; you'd see him in the *Ship Inn*, always in the jug and bottle. He lived opposite the school in Mermaid Street."

The *Martinet* slipped on the blocks during construction and the big shipwright, in trying to get a prop under her, was crushed to death.

"The ship hit him and smashed his brain in," said Henry, cuffing his forehead with his palm. "He was buried up in Rye cemetery," he continued, "never 'ad no gravestone; he spent it as he got it, same as his father." As the identity of anyone buried in an unmarked grave disappears into obscurity, Henry's memory, too, has erased the unfortunate man's name. In contrast, the name of the *Martinet* was never to be forgotten.

She might have now earned the stigma of being a killer but she was a stout ship, as were all the ships launched by G. and T. Smith. "The timber would lay four or five years," declared Harry. "There was never no bit of sap in those planks. You had to fit it properly because men's lives depended on it out at sea." The same care went into the spars. Once a tree is cleaned of bark it is hard to tell which end was rooted into the ground. Harry's way of determining which was the right way up was to stick a pin in a knot hole. "All branches grow up to the light. The pin twists only one way, copying the branch. The way it points is the top of the tree." He explained: "You got to get the tree up the right way, otherwise it would shear off at sea and drown the bloody lot of 'em."

The *Martinet* was to claim another victim before her launching.

A shipwright had been working in a party on one side of the ship that had finished their particular task before the work party on the other side. He fully expected to go and slake his thirst in the pub but the owners ordered him to help out the party who had not yet completed their work.

So disgusted was he that he grabbed the nearest adze without carefully looking first to make sure it was his own. Adzes are very crude-looking tools, but they are more accurate and provide a better finish than a mechanically adjustable smoothing plane. These flat-headed "axes" are like extensions of their users' arms and peculiar to their particular shipwright. This unlucky man had grabbed the wrong tool and with one hefty swing missed the timber he was aiming for and half-crippled himself as the adze smashed into his leg.

The men of Rye were glad to see the stern of the *Martinet* and did not rest until her topsail disappeared down river behind the sedge of the sea wall.

Still the stories passed from mouth to mouth around the coast and her adventures were known by all members of the maritime fraternity of Rye. Her third victim was Captain George Carter, who with his mate Bert Foster took a freight of railway lines to Newhaven. Mysteriously, the wire bond lifting a bundle of the heavy steel rails out of her hold slipped just as Captain Carter walked underneath on his way along the deck. He was killed instantly as the lines rained down on him.

The boomie barge *Martinet* lying deep-loaded off Southend.   *Tony Farnham collection*

Thirteen years before Bob and Bully stepped aboard the *Martinet* she made the headlines again. The *Fishing News* carried the following item in its edition dated 6th March, 1926:

ACCIDENT AT SEA
Windlass Breaks Adrift
SKIPPER AND TWO OF THE CREW INJURED

One of those episodes not uncommon at sea occurred when the Goole ketch Martinet [she was registered at that port] was off Aldeburgh on the Suffolk coast.

All hands were helping to raise the anchor when the windlass was carried away. Captain Burridge had one arm dislocated and almost torn from its socket, another man named Moore sustained a broken kneecap, and a third had his face gashed and got two black eyes. As soon as possible distress signals were hoisted, which were answered by the London barge Britisher and the Walton lifeboat. The captain of the Britisher put his mate on the Martinet to take charge of the vessel.

Captain Burridge, who was in great agony, was placed in a fast motor-boat and landed at Woodbridge to be conveyed to hospital. A tug summoned from Yarmouth towed the Martinet to that port, where Moore was met by a motor ambulance and conveyed to Yarmouth Hospital.

Captain Burridge later died from his injuries. By 1930 the *Martinet* had another skipper, Barney Seaman. The third hand with him was Fred "Bimbo" Mackie, who many years later was to sail with Bob.

Once Barney Seaman and his crew rode out a heavy gale in Corton Roads, losing two anchors. They bent on a spare anchor and days later were trying to save their tide into Margate pier. It was a Friday and the crew were keen to get ashore.

Over the years the huge gaff jaws on the *Martinet* had worn a notch in the mainmast. Usually a roll was kept in the mainsail to keep the jaws clear of the depression. At this time, the procedure for lowering the mainsail was to let the main halyard go first, followed by the peak. This jerked the outward end of the gaff closer to the vertical and dislodged the jaws from the worn part of the mainmast.

On this voyage the wind was fresh, the tide was rapidly ebbing, and in the panic to get her alongside Margate pier the wrong set of halyards were cast off. The gaff jammed in the mast. Barney ordered the anchor to be dropped but the new anchor's shackle jammed in the hawse. Fred takes up the story: "We raced towards the pier and *Martinet* pushed her bowsprit through the crane window. The tension on the topmast stay brought the topmast over like a bow. It only sprang back after the bowsprit snapped.

"You could hear Barney all over Thanet, never mind Margate."

The silhouette of the lofty *Martinet* riding to her buoy at Greenhithe was ignored by the crews of F. T. Everard and Sons. No one wanted to ship aboard her. She was rumoured to be haunted by "Old Carter" and she was old-fashioned even then. Her gear was poor, with patched sails and leaky hull.

In spite of this Bob adored her. She had the magnificent lines of the schooners he so admired and her reputation refused to worry him. Stepping aboard he said, "Don't forget I'll kill you before you kill me."

On reflection Harry Bottreill, who transferred with Bob, thought her reputation unfair. "I did not think there was much evil about her. The windlass was the centre of most accidents on account of the teeth on the pawl gear being so far apart and having only one pawl. This meant if the barge sat back on the chain, particularly in a swell, with the chain short, the handles could fly back about a third of a turn. This made heaving up the anchor a tricky and dangerous business. The *Martinet's* windlass was designed to be power-driven, and if the owners had replaced it with a barge windlass most of the injuries would never have occurred. However, such was the *Martinet's* reputation that whatever accident happened on board, no matter how slight, it added to her bad reputation."

All the talk in the *White Hart* at Greenhithe was of this "new bloke from the schooners" taking the *Martinet*.

Very soon, with some smart passages to Poole to load clay behind him, Bob appeared to the rest of the bargemen at Greenhithe to have tamed the demon

The deck of the *Martinet*, looking aft to the wheel shelter.   *Mrs Sheila Roberts*

ship. He was making good passages and scoffing at the rumours, until one day they went to heave up the anchor while she was lying off Ramsgate waiting for the flood into the Thames.

The pawls are teeth which act like a large ratchet to prevent the windlass barrel being turned the wrong way by the strain of the cable. On the *Martinet* the gaps between these teeth were too great, as Harry explained. As the *Martinet's* bow rose to a sea the chain snubbed, and the winch handles flew back half a circle before the pawls stopped them, knocking both Harry and the third mate, known as Long Bert, flying. Harry recovered but Long Bert's head had to be bandaged to stop the bleeding. On returning to Greenhithe he was taken to hospital.

It was Bob's turn next. Sailing to Wells in Norfolk with oil cake from London, he noticed part of the lacing holding the mainsail head to the gaff had chafed through and was coming adrift. Bob went aloft, watched by his mate at

Left: The *Martinet* towing up the Yare, with the lighter *Quartz* astern, after a particularly rough voyage from London during which the main gaff broke as she entered the Hewett Channel, an entrance to Yarmouth Roads. *Mrs Sheila Roberts*

Below: Alongside the mills in Norwich at the end of the trip upriver. The pieces of the broken gaff can be seen lying on deck; the jaws are still attached to the mast by the parrels. *Mrs Sheila Roberts*

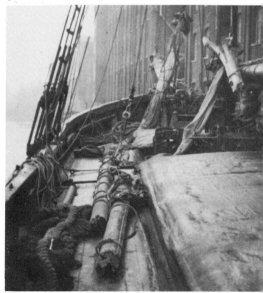

the wheel. He was rather contemptuous of Harry's inability to get higher than the cross-trees.

He clambered out along the gaff and, sitting astride it eighty feet above the deck, began to re-reeve the lacing. Suddenly the gaff took a dip and threw Bob off. Fortunately his hand caught in the lacing he had just replaced, holding him until he could clamber back on the spar. As he climbed down the ratlines Bob was ready to give the new cook a verbal keelhauling, for he thought the man had been meddling with the peak halyard unwittingly. However, when Bob inspected the halyard winch he found the pawl had snapped off. Only the topsail had been holding up the gaff.

If that was not enough of the barge's tricks for one trip, Bob had more to come. During the return voyage he slipped on deck while letting a leeboard down and two fingers of his right hand jabbed into the leeboard winch. The top of one was cut off, the other mashed. Harry bandaged on the severed piece of finger and it "grew" back on.

Bob had a month off on thirty shillings (£1.50) a week.

He had not been back afloat long when, anchoring in fog one morning off the Yantlet Flats in Sea Reach, the *Martinet* was rammed by the motorship *Prowess*, skippered by Barney Seaman. His legendary remark as he looked at his old ship from the bows of the *Prowess* made Bob and Harry laugh, even though they were the ones now burdened with the luck of the *Martinet*. "Well, I'll go to hell if it isn't the old *Martinet*. For ten years I tried to run away from her and now she comes after me in a fog."

The *Prowess* was one of Everards' motorships and there was nothing for it but for her to tow the leaking *Martinet* to Greenhithe. She was repaired on the yard, but corners were still being cut. After all, she was an anachronism in the eyes of her owners, and no money was forthcoming for new spars or sails. On a trip from London to Yarmouth the *Martinet* was caught in a southerly gale. During a gybe the gaff broke in two and the mainsail was carried away.

With the outbreak of war Bob, like many others, anticipated an invasion by the Germans. For some time he had been convinced he would die.

An attractive young blonde nurse, a friend of Cis's, had been visiting his parents' home. She worked at the same hospital at Cis, Southampton General. Her name was Amelia, but she was always known as Toni. Bob's uncertainty as to his fate coupled with the good looks of Toni forged a rather hasty marriage in 1940. They honeymooned in Lyme Regis, going for long walks along the beach behind the barbed wire and black stakes that faced the waves of the threatening Channel. They bought a home in Bexley, just a bicycle ride from the Everard yard at Greenhithe.

Harry said: "Bob just told me casually as we sat below that he'd got married. I'd never met the girl but when I did it was obvious she thought a hell of a lot of Bob and he thought a hell of a lot of her."

Life at sea now came under the dogmatic requirements of Naval Control. Bob had to go along and report to this authority, and received a taste of the optimistic naïveté that was so shocking for civilians when they had their first experience of the military.

Harry recalled him returning with yards of instructions, a .303 rifle and two clips of ammunition. "He put the rifle on the locker and said, 'You know what we've got to do with that?' I said, 'I suppose we're expected to use it if necessary.' He opened up all these papers and read out: 'If you are attacked by enemy aircraft put up a curtain of fire.' Then he said: 'Have you ever heard anything so bloody silly? With this bloody thing, put up a curtain of fire?'"

Bob had asked the Naval officer, "What do you expect us to do, hang up a hatch cloth and set fire to it?"

Harry said: "Bob called them a lot of bloody fools who were going to give us a lot of trouble. He said he didn't mind them telling us where mines were and that sort of thing but they shouldn't interfere with us because none of them

The *Martinet's* broken gaff still aloft as she is towed into Yarmouth by the paddle tug *United Service* one morning in 1939.

Mrs Sheila Roberts

could sail anyway. He could not tolerate the officialdom. He'd rant and rave about it."

Bob was already biased against the Naval control. Another old barge skipper, Bert Fry, had told him what they were like in the First World War, and Bob had a healthy respect for history.

Bert had been just a lad of thirteen and was third hand on the coasting barge *Beatrice Maud*, loaded with guano in sacks from London and bound down Channel for Chichester. On this particular day off Folkestone there was not a breath of wind and the *Maud* was drifting along, her sails like huge slack theatre curtains.

"An examination boat hailed us," said Bert, "and ordered us to heave to as he was coming aboard. We had no steerage way anyway but the skipper made some cosmetic turns of the wheel and the chap came aboard. He asked us what cargo we were carrying, but before anybody could answer he ordered a hatch to be taken off. When he saw the sacks he ordered one to be cut open. 'What is it? Looks like gunpowder to me,' he told the skipper, who was my father, Alfred. Dad said, 'Taste it'. He did so and spat it out. 'What is it?' he asked again. Dad replied, 'Shit'."

As the war took over everybody's world it was the response of Ernie Everett, landlord of the *Theobald's Arms* at Grays in Essex, to the barmy queries from the nation's war machine that impressed Bob the most. It was a reply Bob repeated for the rest of his life and became one of the crown jewels in his prized repertoire.

Ernie, known to all as "Banger", was asked if he could swim when he enlisted for the Royal Navy. "Wot, ain'tcha got no boats?" was his immortal reply.

News came that Henry Trefusis had joined the Royal Naval Volunteer Reserve and had been stationed at Greenhithe on the *Conway*. When they next arrived at Greenhithe Bob was keen to get ashore and see his old shipmate again. There was no room to anchor on the Greenhithe side of the river; they brought up on the north side and Harry dropped Bob off at the *Conway*. Later that night he returned to pick up Bob and was met by Henry, who told him that Bob had drunk a whole bottle of rum. The pair of them carried him to the boat. Harry said that they dumped him in the boat like a sack of potatoes. "I'd never seen him so drunk; he rarely got pickled."

The river was covered in a thick blanket of fog and Harry took the boat over to the north side, praying none of the hooting ships would hit him. Once alongside the *Martinet* they hauled Bob aboard and put him in his bunk. Later the *Martinet* started dragging. Harry gave her more chain, but she would not stop and he "drudged" her across the river, using the anchor to check her. "There were still ships hooting so I left the riding light up. I could tell we'd crossed the river from the amount of the anchor chain we had down. I gave her thirty fathoms and turned in."

The *Martinet*, her sails neatly furled, lies at anchor off Southend.　　　*Tony Farnham collection*

Next day Harry came on deck to discover they were right off Everards' yard. The cook, blissfully unaware of the night's adventure, commented that the passage they had made in the boat seemed of long duration considering how close was ship to shore.

"Then Bob came on deck," continued Harry. "I didn't say anything to him. He looked round and said, 'How the bloody hell did we get here?' I told him, 'When we got aboard last night it was thick fog as you know, or did you know, and she walked away with her anchor.' He said, 'Oh', and not another word was ever said about that episode. It was never referred to. Nothing more was ever said."

Soon after Harry's first "command" of the *Martinet* he left the barges to go into motorships. He worked out he had been earning an average of fourteen shillings (70p) a week while in sail.

Harry said later: "By now I could see very plainly there was no future in barging. Our freights were getting fewer. We had a chat about it and I told Bob I could no longer live on the smell of an oil rag. He appreciated it and that was that."

Bob continued in the *Martinet* with another yachtsman recruit from the Erith Yacht Club, Jerry Thomason, a man with a Cambridge education. He was soon to get a sight of the *Martinet*'s evil ways. While unloading cotton seed at Southampton Bob was climbing down the quayside ladder when his foot slipped and he dropped down between the side of the ship and the quay, just as the *Martinet* took a lurch into the concrete wall. Bob managed to haul himself clear in time but his boots were nipped between ship and quay.

One August day the *Martinet* was sailing down the East Swin loaded with rice for Yarmouth when a dogfight between British fighter planes and German fighters escorting bombers took place overhead. One German plane spiralled down trailing smoke and crashed into the Barrow Deeps. The German pilot drifted down beneath his parachute, dropping not far from the barge. Such was the feeling of hatred for the men who flew the bombers at the time that the crew of the *Martinet* watched the German struggling beneath his chute, slowly dragging it down with him as he drowned.

Bob's comment was: "He provided his own shroud."

Perhaps his thoughts were lingering on his pregnant wife and the bombed houses in the same street. None of the men on the barge felt any remorse.

Bob Roberts and Harry Bottreill at the pumps as the *Martinet* is towed into Yarmouth one morning in 1939. *Mrs Sheila Roberts*

During bad weather the *Martinet* was beginning to wet her freights if she was loaded to her marks. Her hefty rail was fixed to the deck by metal stanchions. In the dock the swim bows of empty lighters would ride up over the loaded sides of *Martinet*, pushing over the rail, which in turn lifted the covering board (the first plank of the deck which meets the side of the ship). Jerry said: "There was a seam there as wide as a shipwright's rule. We would often spend all night at the pumps and still wet the cargo. A couple of times we wet wheat which we took to Norwich. The chaps unloading mixed it up with the dry stuff. It was a hell of a job to keep the water out of her. She was bloody unseaworthy really."

Orfordness in Suffolk marks the northernmost point of the Thames Estuary. South of it there lies a myriad of submerged and drying sandbanks which provided shelter, if to the weather of a barge, and danger, if down to leeward. Many thousands of barges over the years have anchored up under a weather shore and ridden out a gale of wind. To the north of Orfordness lies the open North Sea with no such banks under which to hide. To many sailormen Orfordness was known as the "bargeman's Cape Horn".

In February, 1941, the *Martinet* sailed from Swanscombe loaded with two hundred tons of cement for Norwich. Bob had reluctantly allowed Jerry to bring his brand new bicycle aboard. The scholarly Jerry wanted to explore the Norfolk city. Bob thought it very unseamanlike to carry a bicycle aboard and had it lashed beside the wheelhouse astern where he could not catch sight of it.

They were anchored under the shelter of the Whiting Bank in Hollesley Bay when the westerly wind backed to the south and began to freshen. It was not a good place to bring up but they had no choice. It was getting dark, and Naval Control regulations dictated that no craft must be under way during the night hours. With the fair wind they could have rounded the ness and carried on to Yarmouth.

During the night the *Martinet* began making more water than they could pump out of her. They had no chance of beaching her as the shores were mined and river entrances were barred at night. There was nothing for it but to send up flares and hope the lifeboat would answer their distress call.

"The Aldeburgh lifeboat came for us at about 7 am. We were only in four fathoms of water so we could have jumped in the rigging. It was quite prosaic really," commented Jerry.

The *Martinet* eventually sank a few hours later but her masts remained poking up above the seas right through the following summer. Jerry tried later, from the next barge Bob skippered, to grapple for his beloved bicycle but without success.

Bob felt uneasy having "killed" the killer. All she had ever given him was a clout from the windlass handle. At any rate, he refused to allow a bicycle aboard a ship again.

CHAPTER ELEVEN

Everards'

THE LONG, white-bearded face of Frederick T. Eberhardt still stares down at the obsequious, the outspoken and the sometimes scared crews of the company he founded. Hanging in reception of F. T. Everard and Sons is the portrait of the man who set the little riverside hamlet of Greenhithe to become a location chattered out on telexes the world over.

Some say he wheeled a handcart loaded with his shipwright's tools into the village, others that he stole his first barge. Whatever the truth, he started the most famous barge yard back in the late eighteen-eighties, changing the German origins of his name during the First World War.

The little brick terrace houses dotted along the shore already reflected the winking starboard hand lighthouse on the Grays shore in their windows. Now between the alleyways that divided them rose the bows of barges. Derricks fought for space with washing lines, railway tracks scarred the high street. Everards' built themselves a brick office with their house flag, quartered diagonally red and white, leaded into the windows.

Up behind the village Everards' had their own housing estate where, with autocratic style, they could organise the domestic lives of their crews as well as their professional duties. Port Avenue with its red signpost and Starboard with its green marked out the fifty-four cosy little houses which were offered on rental to Everards' seamen and yard workers.

Street urchins would come and gaze at the industry within the yard. During the early war years *Veronica* sustained damage and lay on the mud at Greenhithe with the tide running in and out of her. The local boys rigged up a diving board across her main hatch coamings.

One of them was Tony Farnham. "We used the main hold as a swimming pool at high water," said Tony, who later joined Bob as third hand in the *Greenhithe*. "The barge skippers of the Everard fleet were my boyhood heroes. I got very friendly with Bob Roberts and used to watch him splicing ropes and wires aboard the *Greenhithe*. I felt like the youngster in the painting depicting the boyhood of Sir Walter Raleigh."

In 1949 at the age of fourteen young Tony shipped aboard the *Greenhithe*.

"On joining the Greenhithe our first cargo was cement from Johnson's works above Greenhithe down to Colchester," Tony remembers. "On arriving I met up with the other barge mates—there were about four other barges in port with us—and off we went ashore for a drink. We ended up in the local tattooist's, where I had a large sailing ship with seagulls, sun and sea tattooed on my arm—the price, seven and sixpence. I had only a half-crown, so I paid the rest with a five-bob seaman's meat coupon—he was real pleased as we got double rations while in the home trade."

Bob's comments on giving up a good meat coupon for a tattoo on Tony's arm were caustic. One day, though, Bob was very pleased when he persuaded a butcher to let them have a joint of beef. It was the third hand's job to cook dinner, and Tony went for'ard to stoke up the range in the fo'c'sle for the crew's Sunday roast.

"Bob told me there were two cans of oil in the fo'c'sle—one contained paraffin for the navigation lamps, the other cooking oil."

Unfortunately for Tony he lovingly basted the meat in paraffin.

Soon clouds of smoke billowed out of the scuttle.

"All I could hear was Bob's voice shouting: 'Christ we're alight', then a bucket of water came swooshing down the fo'c'sle. After shouting and bawling at me, Bob eventually saw the funny side of it, though we had to make do with a tin of bully beef."

Young Tony was certainly thrown in at the deep end of coasting. The mate

The steel barge *Greenhithe*, which Bob Roberts took over after the sinking of the *Martinet*, can be seen on the left of this photograph of the Thames at Greenhithe in the nineteen-thirties.

Tony Farnham collection

Mr Fred Everard and Mr Will Everard on board the committee steamer during a Thames barge match. *Tony Farnham collection*

at the time was Joe Bowler, a fisherman's son. Joe was a good hand but suffered dreadfully from seasickness. The pair of them were aboard the *Greenhithe* when she loaded bulk linseed at Colchester for Hull. Off Cromer the weather thickened from the north-east and Bob was haunted by the fate of the *Hibernia*, which was wrecked on the adjacent coast in the same conditions. So after some ninety-odd miles towards their destination the *Greenhithe* was put about and blown away downwind to the safety of Harwich harbour.

Another time the *Greenhithe* spent six days anchored in Yarmouth Roads awaiting a window in the weather to enter. Tony said, "Bob told us to stow everything up tight, put extra gaskets on sails and batten everything down. We even dropped the topmast and bent on guyropes to the standing rigging. The

69

seas broke right across the barge, the wind screamed through the gear and rigging."

As the days went by stores diminished. "Towards the end we had only flour and potatoes, then only flour, so it was cold dumplings with jam for breakfast and hot dumplings with Oxo for dinner until at last Bob opened the emergency rations (kept in the locker appropriately named the 'Yarmouth Roads') of ships' biscuits and Navy rum."

Frederick Eberhardt's four children, Alf, Will, Fred and Ethel, had the four biggest spritsail barges ever built launched in their names. The four steel monsters were built by Fellows at Great Yarmouth in 1925 and 1926.

Bob now had another of the company's barges, also steel but not as large. The *Greenhithe* had also been built at Fellows' yard, in 1923. Bob had joined the barge in Yarmouth with Jerry coming along as mate. The *Greenhithe's* steel sides had proved too much for her skipper, George Dray, who suffered bronchial trouble. His son, George junior, said: "The *Greenhithe* done him. Being steel she ran with water. Bob was a younger man, he took over in Yarmouth when they carried my old man off." George senior later died from bronchitis. He had an unfortunate end in the *Greenhithe*, losing a suit of sails and having to beach her at Yarmouth. She was towed into the port, her oil cake was discharged, she was patched up and loaded again for Wells. However, off Cromer she blew out the second suit of sails and had to return to Yarmouth.

George saw Bob as an "interloper" in the barging scene but in his poor condition, which led to Bob taking his command, perhaps his view was slightly coloured. Bob's passage-making went from strength to strength as he now had another motive to make as much money as possible. His wife Toni gave birth to a little blonde-haired girl, Anne, in April, 1941.

On one occasion the *Greenhithe* was bound to Yarmouth with 180 tons of cement from London. The barge was hailed off Harwich by the Naval Control examination boat in the late afternoon. All craft were obliged to anchor during the night as part of wartime curfew restrictions. With a fair wind pushing the *Greenhithe* along at a cracking rate of knots the last thing Bob wanted was to have to bring up, so he told the examination boat the barge was bound for Bawdsey, just an hour's sail further on in the entrance to the River Deben. Satisfied the *Greenhithe* would be in port by nightfall, the Navy men allowed Bob to proceed. By the time the darkness had swallowed any trace of the *Greenhithe* she was well on her way round Orfordness.

When the flood tide came against them they anchored off Orford Haven. The next day a storm hit them from the west and the *Greenhithe*, under foresail and half mainsail alone, slashed off downwind towards Holland. They crossed

The mulie barge *Greenhithe* before the wind in the River Thames, July, 1949. The mizzen is brailed up.
Tony Farnham collection

70

The *Greenhithe* at Yarmouth, with the little tug *Gensteam* alongside preparing for the tow up the Yare to Norwich.   *National Maritime Museum*

the mine barrier laid to protect British ships from German attackers. Bob later admitted it was the worst situation in which he had ever been while at sea.

Jerry recalled: "The wind brought up the water. It was a hell of a high water. We lost all the ropes off the hatches, and the boat and the lifebuoys; the flares from the lifebuoys went popping and spewing away along the deck. Waves completely covered the main hatch. Eventually Bob chanced her on the other gybe and we clawed back inshore. But we didn't wet an inch of that cement. Bob said he hoped the foresail would go over without blowing out. It did, and with the ebb under our bow we got to shore. At Aldeburgh the lifeboat came out and asked if we were all right."

Mr Will had been told of the *Greenhithe's* impending doom and had alerted the Royal Air Force and ships in the area. He was impressed when Bob reached Yarmouth of his own accord.

Jerry said: "Bob was getting famous. Bill was extremely keen on the sailing barges and Bob was sailing round all the old boys. Bill was a hard businessman but he was always keen on the sailing barges and he wanted Bob. He knew where all his ships were, where they were heading and what they had in them."

Indeed, at his Greenhithe home in the High Street, a large detached dwelling called Accuba House, the wallpaper over his bed was frayed and marred by a frenzied graffiti of telephone numbers. Coastguards, agents, merchants, tug-owners, all were scribbled next to his bed. When Mr Will could not sleep he would ring up and find out where his ships were.

Everard, because he got his ships about, had the command of the coast. Bargemen could sit about for weeks on North Woolwich Buoys if they were in Sully's or Goldsmiths' barges; not so with Everards'. His men were always sure of a good living, if they did not drown earning it first. Bob secretly admired Mr Will and was impressed with his cavalier style.

When the *Greenhithe* was cut down and sunk in the Thames by a steamship taking troops to France, Mr Will was on hand.

Jerry described what happened: "The ship was coming down on our port quarter. We put a board across the river to keep out of his way, then the silly bloody idiot came on our starboard side. We had just come about and had no way on when the ship took the wind from our sails. Bob could see it was inevitable he would hit and was worried the sprit would fall and injure his wife and daughter who were with us."

Jerry got Toni and Anne into the barge boat, and as the rammed *Greenhithe* turned over on her beam ends Bob and Ginger Calver, the third hand, dived off her side. Mr Will, who took delivery of a new Rolls Royce every year and had the dimple buttons on the back seats cut out and the seams re-stitched by his sailmaker, Alf Naylor, because they were not to his fancy, collected the shipwrecked mariners and had them driven to their respective homes in the car—chauffeur driven.

Jerry said: "It was typical of him."

The *Greenhithe* was salvaged and taken back up river to Everards' yard. Bob was summoned to the City office in Fenchurch Street to meet the two active members of the firm, Mr Fred and Mr Will. He was offered a motorship. It was 1944 and Everards' were building up the biggest fleet of coasting ships in the United Kingdom. Bob refused, explaining he had been in sail all his life and was not willing to throw away all the knowledge he had gathered. He said he would look for another company with another barge. Mr Will seemed relieved there was somebody with the sailing barges at heart and Mr Fred promised to refit the *Greenhithe*.

Jerry thought Bob had made a mistake. "It was a bloody tragedy. He hung on to sailing too long. He could have had a motorship with a good salary and would have made a damn good skipper. He was a superb seaman." Bob's days in power were a long way off yet.

Jerry told Bob that he would not live on the £2 15s (£2.75) a week yard pay while the *Greenhithe* was brought back to life and he left, taking the sailing barge *Jane* as master. For Bob it was a sad blow, but he was also very proud that he had turned a yachtsman into a fully fledged barge skipper.

For three months that summer Bob relieved Jimmy Uglow, another of

The *Greenhithe* in Sea Reach, outward bound from the Thames after undergoing repairs following a machine-gun attack off the Suffolk coast during the Second World War.

74

Everards' skippers and a man who had a name in the company as a "top chaser", in the *Will Everard*. He was impressed with her sheer size. She was, after all, nearly one hundred tons bigger than the *Greenhithe*. Bob tried everything in the *Will*, all points of sailing, setting everything she had to set. For Captain Uglow was the senior skipper, the "Don" of Everards' with twelve years' more experience in the company than Bob.

When the *Greenhithe* was eventually re-launched in 1945 Bob shipped back aboard with a young man from Yarmouth as mate. Jack Woods had a mop of hair like rich coils of bass rope, yellow bass rope, which gained him the nickname "Blondie".

Blondie described the *Greenhithe*: "She was too tender for when that blew.

Arthur "Benny" Bennett and, in the background, Chris Alston at work in Everards' sail loft at Greenhithe. Many barge sails were made and repaired here. *Tony Farnham collection*

She was all right in smooth water but when there was a bit of wind we used to carry more water on deck than we did over the side. But old Bob he was the only bargeman I ever knew who'd heave to. If that come on bad he'd claw off the land and leave the bowline on the fores'l and heave to.

"He was a stickler for his gear. There was no loose ends aboard, no Irish pennants."

Once the *Greenhithe* nearly capsized. Blondie was below having his dinner when Bob shouted at him to get on deck and help him with the wheel. A squall hit the barge and Bob said, "Christ, she's going over, up helm, up helm." Blondie was under water in the lee side of the wheelhouse but the *Greenhithe* staggered up again. As Blondie came out of the sea he was ordered to down helm again. "She was streaming ropes and anchor chain and everything astern on us," said Blondie. "We didn't touch a sheet or nothing, that blew so hard."

On one trip the *Greenhithe* had discharged coal at Harwich when they received orders to sail to Colchester and load straw for Ridham Dock in Kent. It was a poor freight used in making newsprint for the daily newspapers. The pair were even more irritated when they got news that Jimmy Uglow in the *Will Everard* was loading wheat in London for Yarmouth. Wheat was a well-paid freight.

Instead of sailing into the Colne, Bob and Blondie sailed on to Greenhithe, where they were met by Mr Will.

Blondie said: "He told us there was no freight for us in the London River and he ordered us to load coal in Keadby up the River Trent and we were to sail there light. That was Bill Everard being damned awkward."

That was a hell of a long passage, up round the coast of Norfolk, past the Wash and up the Humber into South Yorkshire, to make unloaded and therefore unpaid. Mr Will would not suffer any insubordination and when Bob and Blondie refused to do it they were sacked. "But", Mr Will told them, "you can't leave until you've got to Keadby."

One consolation of the long haul to Keadby was the *New Friendship Inn* situated near the coal chute from which the barges were loaded. This pub was one of the handful of hostelries which took the bargemen to its heart. The welcome they received was warm, the food plentiful, the beer served at any time of day or night and the credit generous. Often beer slates would be run up and not paid off for months, not until the next time the barge arrived on the Trent.

All the crews knew and loved the little, dark-haired bar tender, George "Ikky" Drakes. He earned his nickname from the way he parted his black hair. The landlady thought he looked like Hitler, or Ikky, as she pronounced the name.

George declared that Bob was one of the finest men you could ever meet. "He was always laughing."

However, there was one source of merriment which irritated George: "Bob

Albert and Lila Spriggs and "Ikky" the barman at the *New Friendship Inn* at Keadby, up the Trent.
The welcome they gave to bargemen was warm, the food was plentiful and the credit generous.

would come in, order a pint, then leave it on the bar and go and sit at a table. He
would then ask me to bring it over and when I got to the table he would give a
little bark and his bloody dog would leap up from under the table and bite my
ankle. He thought it was hilarious."

Bob and Blondie philosophically decided to sail the *Greenhithe* to Keadby as
Mr Will had ordered. On arrival at the coaldust-speckled village there was a
letter waiting from Miss Ethel. In it was £5 each, payment "for sailing light". A
diplomatic lesson was learnt. Nobody told Mr Will what to do or disobeyed
orders. They loaded coal for Harwich and on returning to London River were
fixed with wheat to Yarmouth. Nothing more was said about the sack.

CHAPTER TWELVE

Captain Jimmy Uglow

THE BIG man with long "bacon rasher" ears drove his barge *Will Everard* as Neptune drove his white horses. He had been bombed, he had often narrowly escaped being wrecked, but through the howling tempest which sometimes cowed his crews Jimmy Uglow sang arias from *La Bohème* while wrestling with the wheel, his black trilby whipped by spindrift.

Bob and he became great, sometimes bitter, rivals. It was commonplace for mates on the *Greenhithe* and the *Will* to find themselves engaged in frantic races as their skippers tried to hide a heartbeating anticipation of getting to a destination first under a gentlemanly cool demeanour. Anchor pawls would be lifted from the windlass to prevent their telltale clinking drifting across to the ears of the crew in the other barge. Like ghost ships, the two barges would get under way with only their riding light for illumination. Jimmy flew in the face of all superstition to get his passage before Bob. He sailed regardless on Friday the thirteenth. The fearless barge skipper became morose only when his cigarettes ran out. As he neared port he cheered up visibly at the thought of a pint and a smoke, especially if he was in the bar before Bob.

Sometimes his elation at beating the *Greenhithe* led to one or two pints over the top. Albert Butterfant, who sailed with him as mate, remembers Jimmy clunking on the *Will's* steel decks in the early hours draped in a white sheet in an attempt to haunt his crew, but Jimmy did not require any props to scare the living daylights out of those who sailed with him. Once he knew the *Greenhithe* was anywhere in the vicinity nothing would stop him.

On one occasion the *Will* picked up her anchor off Shoebury on a bitterly cold night. It had hooked up a loop of chain and fouled itself. Jimmy sent the mate for'ard with the third hand to clear it. After an hour they still had not done it. He bellowed for the mate to come aft to the wheel, then said, "Let somebody who knows what they're doing have a go."

He used the small length of bowsing chain on the rail to take the weight of the anchor, then slacked away on the main cable, climbed out on to the anchor fluke and cleared it. Just as he did so the bowsing chain snapped and Jimmy, anchor and all, plunged into the icy waters of the Thames. The bowsprit was topped up and Jimmy grabbed the bobstay, which was running up and down the stem, as he plummeted. The anchor stopped short below the foot of the stem and Jimmy disappeared under water. He was standing on the stock with his nose squashed against the stem at water level as the barge surged forward under a freshening breeze.

Jimmy takes up the story: "I heard the third hand say, 'The skipper's gorn.' I think he sounded pleased. He shouted again, 'The skipper's gorn.' And a voice from sea-level said, 'No he hasn't, you little bastard. Get the mate along and heave this anchor up.'"

After that episode Jimmy seemed invincible. The story went round the coast with an added underwater journey which took Jimmy the length of his barge and had him crawling up the rudder and over the stern to cut short his crew's celebratory dancing!

At the time Bob had a young man called George Dray, son of the George Dray Bob had relieved in the *Greenhithe*, sailing with him as third hand. Young George knew his father had sailed with Jimmy and he had slightly resented Bob taking over his father's barge. George asked Jimmy if he could sail with him in the *Will*. Both barges were in the Millwall Dock at the time and Jimmy told

Captain Jimmy Uglow.
Tony Farnham collection

George he would have to finish his round trip with Bob first and then apply. He did so and left the *Greenhithe*.

Jimmy said: "Bob accused me of stealing him, and the ill feeling started." What made matters worse was the fact that Mr Will held Jimmy as his favourite among the bargemen. Jimmy recalls: "I remember Bob laying on the buoys empty and we got orders to load a second freight. I said it hardly seemed fair with Bob laying empty. But Mr Will told me, 'You can't get a quart into a pint pot, she's only 160 tons. Anyway I shouldn't concern yourself about Roberts, he certainly doesn't concern himself about you.' It was all cut-throat. He deliberately used to set you against each other; that made sure you got a fast passage. It was his policy."

This policy provided the competition and excitement between them, if any more was required. According to Jimmy: "Bob was so determined to get the better of me, we had one or two damn good sails." In his great white barge Jimmy seemed to Bob like the elusive Moby Dick, always just that half a mile ahead, or just a few minutes before Bob getting the tug. On one trip, when both barges were bound from the London River for Great Yarmouth, Jimmy put the *Will* ashore off Southend on a falling tide. "There was an eight-hour gap between us and Bob got there first. He was very proud of himself. But that was the last time he ever beat the *Will Everard*."

Jimmy's revenge was not long in coming. The *Will* was coming out of Harwich. There was a fine south-westerly breeze and two miles off he saw the *Greenhithe* empty and bound for Keadby.

The chase began.

Both barges worked every tide and the *Will* narrowly beat the *Greenhithe* into the berth at Keadby. The barges loaded and towed down to Hull together. The race was now set to get back to Colchester. "We were turning away down, long and short boards. I knew Bob was on our weather quarter, so I thought I'd try a little trick. I told the crew to let go the jib and flying jib when I hollered out 'lee-o', then let her fill again and make them fast on the same tack. Bob saw the headsails loosen and promptly went on the other tack." Jimmy turned in, leaving his mate at the wheel. He was later awakened by flapping canvas. "I came on deck to find this goon hadn't trimmed the sails properly and Bob was a quarter of a mile ahead on my weather. We were off Orfordness and the tide was done. I worked inshore to Felixstowe. Bob stayed out by the Roughs Tower. I tacked up the Wallet and got ahead of him again."

Back aboard the *Greenhithe* the new mate, Ivan Hazelton from Ipswich, was swinging round the rigging like a trapeze artist. The *Greenhithe's* weather crosstree had buckled under the press of canvas, and to Bob's fury they had been forced to lower the staysail. Ivan had rummaged out a length of thick wire from the fo'c'sle, shackled one end on the end of the crosstree, then sweated up the other end on the leeboard winch. Then they set the staysail again. It was to no

The *Will Everard* at the Hythe, Colchester. Although the photograph was taken after the war she still retains a bullet-proof extension to the wheelhouse.   *Roger Finch*

use. The giant *Will Everard* was the first to anchor in the River Colne off Brightlingsea.

Jimmy added: "I told the mate I was turning in but ordered him to stay up and wait for Bob to come in. I said, 'Make sure you shout out goodnight Bob so that he knows who's who.'" Bob later asked Jimmy's permission to include the race, which turned out to be the last between two sailing coasters, in his own written account. "I just dropped a postcard back and told Bob to do as he liked as long as he remembered we beat him both ways, and I never heard no more."

It had been an 180-mile race, and Bob had lost by just two miles.

Jimmy could not help but admire Bob's determined efforts to unseat him for the Everard "throne". "He was the type of man that Everard was always looking for. He would risk anything to get passage and that was Everards' ideal. Funny thing, in many ways I liked old Bob. He was very good company, especially ashore; a bit coarse, but he could mix with anybody . . . if only he hadn't got that bee in his bonnet about me."

They joined together to fight one enemy, the Naval Control during the war. Once off Yarmouth the *Will Everard* and the *Greenhithe* were towing astern of the harbour tug when they fouled a minefield trot, a number of mines moored in a prearranged pattern. According to Albert Butterfant, the tug crew went aft, and Bob and Jimmy went ashore to drink off the shock.

Before the Naval party arrived to arrest the offenders Jimmy hastily got out his chart covering that sea area. He had not bothered to affix the alteration

When racing, the *Cambria* set extra sails to take full advantage of a light following wind.
Thames Barge Sailing Club collection

provided by the Naval Control, which showed the minefield, to the chart. This he now did and all hands were called to smudge their thumbs on the new square of chart to make it seem well consulted!

The great barge races provided further opportunities for Jimmy and Bob to show their mettle. Initially Bob crewed aboard the *Sara*, though later he had his chance at the helm of his own barge.

During one of the matches when Bob was crewing in the *Sara* Tony took Anne aboard the paddle steamer *Medway Queen* to follow the race. *Sara* crossed tacks at close quarters with another barge on the port tack. Language was getting strong. Suddenly a voice louder than the others said to the port tacking barge, "Get the eff out of it." Little Anne turned proudly and said loudly to her mum, "That was my daddy!"

The tactic for such close sailing was to send a man out on the end of the bowsprit and when on port tack the barge stood on ". . . until he could gob down the other helmsman's neck, then you wind her," Bob explained to a friend.

When he did have the opportunity of sailing his own barge in the Thames match of 1955 it was as master of Everards' coaster *Cambria*, which had won the coaster class on both Thames and Medway on her previous appearance in the races in 1938. She was a working barge rigged for everyday trading, whereas the *Sara*, a barge with a long string of racing successes which had been given to Jimmy, was by then maintained solely for the annual races; she had been laid up at the yard at Greenhithe since the previous year's races.

The *Cambria* and the *Sara* were both sailing in the champion bowsprit class. Fred Cooper, the historian of the barge races, wrote that *Cambria* "looked massive compared with the sleek *Sirdar* and *Sara*, and the light winds were not ideally suited to her heavy hull, but even so she was never entirely out of the race." The *Cambria* arrived at the finish forty-seven minutes after the *Sara*, "the light and variable winds having no doubt been rather exasperating to Bob Roberts and his crew on *Cambria*".

As it turned out both the Everard barges were beaten by the *Sirdar*, the London and Rochester Trading Company entry, which had been completely sheathed with one-inch pine and had been given a new suit of sails specially for the 1955 matches. For one of his skippers to allow himself to be beaten by his hated rivals from the Medway was an unforgivable sin in the eyes of Mr Will. At the end of the race the skippers came aboard the committee boat, where the top executives from the competing companies had been watching the race. If an Everards' man was a winning skipper, Mr Will, Mr Fred and Miss Ethel would buy him a drink and invite him into their company. After the fateful 1955 Thames match there was a cool reception for both Jimmy and Bob.

Jimmy said: "Tom Cook beat us in the *Sirdar*. I clapped when he was handed his cup and said, 'Well done, Tom, fair win.' That was it, all three of them deliberately turned their backs on me and never said a thing."

That year Bob came in a minute and a half after *Dreadnought*, which led the staysail class home, making the *Cambria* the fourth barge to finish. In later years he was to have considerable racing success in the *Dreadnought* after she had been bought by Mr Will Everard. In her he won the staysail class on the Thames in both 1958 and 1959, coming second in the same class on the Medway in those years.

Improvements were made to her rig under her new ownership and in 1960 she was completely re-rigged with a forty-five-foot bowsprit. From then on she raced in the champion bowsprit class on both the Thames and Medway, Bob continuing to command her in the races.

As soon as the flags and fuss of race day were packed away it was back to the grind of earning a living. Back to the endless runs to Yarmouth and its treacherous entrance. The tide always sets on to the north pier, whether on the ebb or the flood. Bob lost two boats in the *Greenhithe*, cracked like nuts as she was swept on to the pier. He then had the davits rigged on the port side instead of the starboard side, as was normal in barges.

In Yarmouth town the crews of the few remaining barges were cutting off ropes' ends and were selling them to rag merchants for beer money, together with waistcoats and odd bits of cloth. That beer money was known as "a weskit

Opposite: The *Sara's* crew for the Thames match of 1957. From left to right they are Tom Willis, Albert Day, Jack Burford, Jimmy Mole, Fred Mackie and Bob Roberts.
Tony Farnham collection

Right: Captain Jimmy Uglow receiving the cup after winning the Coronation Match on the Thames in *Sara*.
Tony Farnham collection

sub" (waistcoat sub). They would dip into each barge's paraffin tank to make up a pint of the stuff and sell that as well. Cow heel and chips was three pennies (1.25p) a packet.

Ivan and the third hand had to whistle if they were making a duff down below while Bob was at the wheel. Ivan said: "He wanted to make sure we weren't eating the currants!"

Given a fair wind there was profit still to be made, but should the breeze start heading the barge, Bob said, "That old fores'l would quiver and we'd have to wind her, then the sail would flog and the sheet'd go 'nuthin-ter-come, nuthin-ter-come.' "

Bob was a tough customer, as Ivan, a small wiry man, found out.

The *Greenhithe* was loading in the King George V Dock for Lowestoft. A big, bragging docker had been calling Ivan a "Suffolk swede" and mimicking his singsong accent. When Ivan told him to shut up the docker climbed out of the hold on to the deck. Bob stood in the way, characteristically pulling his nose and wiping his face, an embarrassed "tic", because he knew what was going to happen.

Ivan said: "Bob swiped him across the face with the back of his hand and knocked him down."

When the *Greenhithe* arrived in Lowestoft the barge misfetched and crashed alongside three Scottish fishing boats, breaking two planks on one of them. It was a Sunday and the fishermen had just returned from church. Ivan said: "They all threw their bibles down on deck before swearing at us."

The *Greenhithe's* fate became apparent on one trip from Keadby to Colchester with coal. She started making a lot of water, and Bob found a wafer-thin plate in the fo'c'sle. He banged a wooden fid through the hole and got the barge to Colchester. Later, at Greenhithe for her load line survey, it was discovered she needed a lot of re-plating. Everards' did not think it worth spending the money.

It was 1951. Once again the company offered Bob a motorship. Once again he refused, but there was no other sailing barge for him to take. The *Cambria* was still sailing but she had a skipper, Frank "Cully" Toevil. The *Will Everard* had been fitted with an auxiliary engine, and Jimmy was none too pleased with the compromise.

"It nearly broke my heart after the first trip with the engine. All the paint was discoloured from oil. And the smoke from the exhaust had eddied around and blacked the white paint on the transom and the rudder.

"In two weeks it looked as if she had not seen a shipyard for two years." Now with his engine, Jimmy was ordered away from Sittingbourne one black night in a south-westerly gale. Under sail he would have stayed in his berth. The *Will Everard* struck the Kingsferry Bridge on her port bow, denting the steel side between two frames.

"I was disgusted with the whole thing, with myself for doing the damage and with Mr Will because of the orders that had caused it. At Greenhithe I reported to Mr Fred; his only remark about the damage was, 'You are bound back there again. See if you can match up the other side.' Thus began the four years out of the twenty-three I was master of the *Will Everard* that I enjoyed least."

The barge did not settle down easily with her "iron topsail". By all accounts it was a poor conversion and Mr Will flew into a rage every time the engine broke down and Jimmy had to regress to sailing, thus risking the deadline his boss had set.

"I was cracking up. I had phlebitis, neuritis. I couldn't sail her any more. He wanted me 365 days a year, twenty-four hours a day, body, mind and soul, because of that damned engine."

Jimmy's sea-cold, lugubrious, green eyes started looking shorewards. He rowed away from the *Will Everard*, walked up through the village of Greenhithe, the village his boss had taken over, and slammed the door of his home. The model his son had made of the *Will* was consigned to the basement. He cleared the large glass showcase in his front room of his racing cups. They too were left to go black in the basement.

CHAPTER THIRTEEN

Pin Mill

THEY had sailed in out of a gale and moored to the old black buoy spattered with cormorant's muck which swirled in the bight of Butterman's Bay. As the topsail dropped into exhausted creases when Bob let go the halyards, his old skipper Percy Quantrill looked aloft and said, "All is safely gathered in," as he often did when the *Oxygen* reached the safety of the River Orwell.

As they rowed the skiff up river to the pebble hard at Pin Mill, Bob became entranced with the deep wooded banks which ran down to the river's edge. Up ahead the yellow lights of the *Butt and Oyster* beckoned, the smoke from its chimneys filtering through the darkening woods behind. Percy invited Bob home for supper at his little house, Rose Cottage. Both men were wary of Mrs Quantrill. May had the dinner ready when she heard "Puccy boy", as her husband was known, had reached Butterman's Bay and her culinary timetable did not allow for a lengthy stay at the pub.

That was in 1937, and ever since that first visit to Pin Mill Bob vowed he, too, would live there one day. He asked Percy to look out for any property coming on the market, and in due course Percy told him of a little cottage just up the lane from his own, Dwiny Cottage.

Bob bought the cottage in 1949 and moved his family round there from Kent by sea. He had for some years owned a hefty Whitstable smack, the *Stormy Petrel*. Two years before moving to Pin Mill Bob had taken Tony and Anne on a sailing holiday aboard the smack from the London River down to Poole. The following year, in February, Tony had given birth to another daughter, Jill, and since that event Bob had not spent much time on the smack.

As a removal van, the *Stormy Petrel* made an incongruous sight as she surged down Swin with rolls of linoleum lashed on deck and Anne's tiny legs dangling through the scuppers kicking at the waves.

It was a proper bargeman's hamlet. Harry King built boats at Pin Mill, Reuben Webb repaired them, and Jack Ward rented out the moorings. Barges were laid up for repairs or breaking on the hard. All this activity took place within full view of the pub. The *Butt and Oyster* was the centre of village life, so much so for the bargemen that irate wives had been known to take their errant husbands' dinners down to them at the pub, slapping the plates on the bar before them in disgust.

The tiny hamlet was flooded on the big spring tides: the river would rush up into the stream, called the grindle, which ran through the gardens of the cottages, swelling it into a tributary of the Orwell and making folk move their things upstairs. Bob built a two-foot-high wall all round his cottage, hoping it would act as a sea defence, but during the floods of 1953 the wall simply kept a moat of water around Dwiny Cottage after the tide had ebbed. Toni, with help from May Quantrill, had to bail the water out on her own because Bob was away at sea.

Bob completely identified with his new Suffolk home. Only a day's sail up the coast was his "ancestral home" of Kessingland where his mother's family had lived.

He cultivated the local characters, and their eccentricities became the best stories told on the coast. There was George "Bunger" Burroughes, for instance. Bunger was the local harbour master. A man of few words but of many pained expressions, mainly in response to the inane requests of visiting yachtsmen.

Perhaps the most famous encounter of Bunger's was with a young city gent who wanted to employ Bunger to take his yacht round to the Solent in preparation for the season's racing. All through the lunch hour the young man

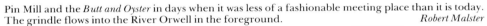

Pin Mill and the *Butt and Oyster* in days when it was less of a fashionable meeting place than it is today. The grindle flows into the River Orwell in the foreground.   *Robert Malster*

appealed to the mute Bunger. The irascible old man opened his mouth only to consume the frequent pints of beer supplied by his client. "Time" was called and Bunger had only one desire, to sheer left outside the door and walk home for his lunch. Instead the young man desperately harried him out to the right and down the hard to inspect the yacht.

Bunger reluctantly trudged down the hard, his eyes scanning the moorings trying to locate the yacht of the confounded city man, but he could see no new craft. Presently he heard the young man calling him and turned round to find him pointing to a sixteen footer, brand new, and almost shoal draught enough to lay afloat in the grindle where she was moored.

With a look of disgust, Bunger uttered his only words of the day, "Put a stamp on it, powst it." Then he went home for lunch.

With the decline in the number of sailing vessels and no suitable craft for him to command Bob left Everards' in 1951 and took a full-time job on a regional morning newspaper, the *East Anglian Daily Times*, as a sub-editor in their offices at Ipswich. He was also writing articles for the yachting magazines. In the same year as he moved to Pin Mill his second book, *Coasting Bargemaster,* was published. A rollicking account of his more dramatic experiences in the barges, it unfairly became known among the cynical Ipswich sailormen as "Boasting Bargemaster".

Bob was becoming very aware of his second-string occupation and more importantly the fact that it was, as he saw it, losing him credibility among the regular seafarers. As a result, he made some token trawling runs in the *Stormy Petrel*, but the catches were not enough to feed the village cat.

Suffolk logic was another aspect of Pin Mill life which delighted Bob. One family, the Sharmans, had plenty of it. Bob's first experience was with grandfather Sharman, who had the wonderful christian name of Ephraim.

The walrus-moustached Ephraim and his grandson Peter were digging a ditch round the grindle to let trapped water run away. Bob, meanwhile, was building a temporary dam in his section of the stream to hold a baby seal he had rescued to the delight of the children. He overheard Ephraim admonishing young Peter for not finishing the crusts of his lunchtime sandwiches. As Peter carelessly tossed away the bread, Ephraim said, "Don't throw they away boy, then when you ain't got none you'll 'ave some."

Another example of the Suffolk way of looking at things was the opinion another old bargeman had of Canada. The small, jet-black-haired Spiro Ling had eventually been persuaded to visit one of his sons who had settled there. He was worried about leaving Suffolk, for he felt he might have to be buried outside his beloved county should the grim reaper strike while he was away, but visit he did. When he returned Bob asked him what he thought of Canada. "Well", said Spiro, supping a pint, "that's a wonderful place. You can go to the top of a mountain and see for 'undred miles, but there ain't nothin' to look at."

For Bob there was always plenty to look at as he sailed up the Orwell. His imagination was full of the smuggling stories he had either read or been told, and from the deck of a barge he would recount them as he passed a particular point in the river.

How the excise men would bury themselves up to their necks in the shingle waiting for smugglers to come ashore and how one was once shot dead as he leapt out of his hole. How Margaret Catchpole, the moll of smuggler Will Laud, was sent to Australia for stealing a horse to visit her man; she lived opposite Pin Mill at Nacton Heath. Just upstream from Pin Mill on the same side of the river is a place called the Cat House. It was here that Will Laud watched for the sign indicating all was well, that there were no excise men about. The sign was a cut-out silhouette of a cat set in the window in front of a light. If the cat was not there, the contraband was not landed.

All the poetry of the past and the weekend "fishing" in the *Stormy Petrel* could not eradicate the nagging fact in Bob's mind that he was a newspaper man again, working regular hours.

The very year Bob left Everards' he accepted the offer of a trip across the North Sea. Even his doubts about machine-driven ships could not keep him away from the opportunity of bringing the sixty-seven-foot twin-engined cruiser *Gowan Brae* back to Harwich from Holland. She had been on charter to Dutch holidaymakers. The owner, Douggie Burns, would be "engineer" and a retired colonel, A. S. Tibb, who was a day off his seventieth birthday, was also aboard.

About fifty miles east of Harwich the owner dashed on deck telling Bob the engine room was ablaze. They tried to put out the fire with extinguishers but it had the cruiser in its grip. Bob ordered the anchor to be dropped. He reasoned the westerly wind would keep the cruiser's bow head to wind and stop the flames coming forward, but, in the middle of the North Sea, it took sixty fathoms of chain before the anchor hit the bottom.

All three men had to abandon the cockpit. They climbed up on to the foredeck. They donned their lifebelts and, as the deck became too hot to sit on, they lowered themselves into the sea using the anchor chain. Unfortunately, Colonel Tibb's lifebelt slipped off him. Bob handed him his own. Douggie noticed a passing oil drum in the darkness and swam off to get it for Bob. Colonel Tibb could not stand the cold after an hour of hanging on to the anchor chain and he attempted to climb back aboard. He lost his grip and fell back into the sea, drifting away before Bob could grab him.

Bob later described his experience to a radio reporter: "I was paddling away, I am not a very good swimmer. I thought, 'This is it.' It's funny the things that come to you. You think about the family and the people you know; you're

Captain Harold Robertson aboard the *Redoubtable* with
his mate, Ephraim Sharman.　　*Mr Peter Sharman*

actually talking to them, saying goodbye to them in a voice you don't recognise. It's not your own voice."

Bob had told Colonel Tibb to hang on because there were ships in the vicinity but he said to the reporter, "I hadn't seen any ships; I just said it to encourage him."

With a final explosion the *Gowan Brae* sank. Bob drifted in the darkness until a passing Dutch coaster, the *Tyro*, picked him up. Her master, J. Van der Zwan, had already picked up Douggie but Colonel Tibb was never seen again.

Bob's venture back afloat had hardly divorced him from newspapers. His own ran the story under the headline "It Was Roast Or Drown".

Bob's spell ashore lasted only three years. In 1954 Everards' wrote to him asking him to rejoin the company as master of their last sailing barge in commission, the *Cambria*. Her skipper, Frank "Cully" Toevil, had fallen ill and retired. In the rat-race of Everard employ Cully had got away with slow passages. There had been a time when he was a "chaser", loading two freights a week, but in his latter days he took things more leisurely. The word had it he got away with it because old man Everard, the first, had employed him and always had a soft spot for him. Sometimes, though, he exasperated the more frenetic Mr Will.

Once, after a particularly slow passage to Yarmouth, he sent a telegram to

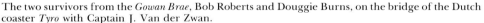

The two survivors from the *Gowan Brae*, Bob Roberts and Douggie Burns, on the bridge of the Dutch coaster *Tyro* with Captain J. Van der Zwan.

Peter Sharman pumping
out *Cambria* in the nineteen-sixties.
Mr Peter Sharman

Everards' to say he had arrived. Mr Will wired back a single word in reply:
"Hooray".

Bob took command of his new ship on 29th October, 1954. He was very
proud of her, for she was a fast barge in very good shape. Picking up the old
buoy in Butterman's Bay, he remembered his early days with Percy and took
under his wing young Peter Sharman, hoping to inspire him with barges the
same way he himself had been awed. Peter became the son Bob never had but
always wanted. When Bob was away on some other business, Peter would scull
down to Butterman's Bay and pump the barge out, sometimes, in her later days,
for as little as £1. "Old Bob would say, 'Nip down and give her a jog out'. One
morning I'd been on the back-breaker for an hour and half and there was still
nine inches of water on the ceiling. It took me five hours to get it all out."

Bob was delighted with Peter's prowess aloft. Peter could slide down the
topsail halyard from the crosstrees, nipping the rope with his feet and stopping
dead just inches before the bottom block. Once in the Royal Albert Dock he was
halfway along the sprit when he fell. Luckily the *Cambria* was uncovered and half
full of maize. Peter had a soft, if dusty, landing.

Another time, lying at Pin Mill, the bottom of the topsail started coming adrift in a gale of wind. Bob asked Peter to nip along and put a second gasket round the wayward canvas. "Not today," replied Peter with his peculiarly Suffolk confidence. Bob sent his mate, Ginger Latham, aloft instead. Peter explained "If I fall you can never get another me but you can always get another Ginger."

During Bob's occasional trips away to Holland in yachts he laid the *Cambria* up on Pin Mill hard. Peter, whose dark good looks had many admirers in the hamlet, made full use of Bob's cabin in his absence. His antics did not go unnoticed, however. The canny George Burroughes did not let much get past him. One summer morning he met young Peter crunching up the hard before breakfast. Realising he was on his way home, George removed the stubby pipe from his mouth to inquire, "Hello Peter, varnished your bowsprit lately?

Behind Bob's blue and white cottage was a long plot of land raging with out-of-control vegetables and windswept beansticks. The wild tangle was witness to the fact that Bob was at sea most of the time once again. However, there was one day of the year when it was sure to get attention if Bob happened to be at home. That day was barge race day. Not barge race day proper, as Bob saw it, but barge racing by the amateurs. Thames barges were beginning to become popular among enthusiasts. They were re-rigging the old craft that had gone out of commission and were even organising their own races. One such race was the Orwell match.

Bob's daughter Jill said later: "Pin Mill barge match is very fraught, but it was the only time we got the garden dug. Dad had his breakfast, then he would get the garden fork and go right up to the end of the garden, and turn his back on the river. He didn't even go down the *Butt*. At the end of the day he put his fork away and didn't get it out until barge race day the following year."

The village was beginning to change. Boatyards became car parks, cottages rented by fishermen and bargemen were being bought by weekending Londoners as their ancient occupants died off.

Bob imagined he heard less of the raucous pheasants he shot in the woods along the shore. "It's those bloody foreigners," he raged, "with their suburban ways. Slamming car doors late at night and screaming goodbye to each other; they've scared them off."

CHAPTER FOURTEEN

And Then There Was One

THE INDUSTRIAL profile of London's river was rarely punctuated now by the cow-brown topsails of barges. By the sixties the *Cambria* had only five other trading barges for company.

Bob was beginning to sense his place in history and in some respects was impatient for the title of last sailorman. Already he was categorising the *Cambria's* companions as short-haul barges. They were not making the longer coasting passages, which left the *Cambria* as the "real" contender to be Britain's last merchant sailing ship. The Ipswich grain barges, R. and W. Paul's *Anglia* and *Marjorie,* with Cranfields' *Spinaway C, Venture* and *May,* were running cereals from London to Ipswich. It was left to the *Cambria* to make the longer runs, up to Keadby on the Trent to load coal for Colchester, and grain to Norwich or cattle cake for Yarmouth.

Mates were becoming harder to keep. Billy Evans married and left the *Cambria* after a year with Bob: "I came ashore. I could see there was going to be no money in it, no future. But Bob got me a job on the yard at Greenhithe."

Bob also typed a letter to Mr Will recommending Billy for a house on the Everard estate. He now kept his typewriter aboard; the pen was proving mightier than the wheel. Billy was allocated number eighteen Port Avenue.

Ironically, as the *Cambria* became unique, Bob's earning power as a scribe increased. He no longer had to tout articles round to the yachting magazines or newspapers. They came to him for material. In 1955, Des Sleightholme from *Yachts and Yachting* shipped aboard the *Cambria* for a trip up from Yarmouth. It was a chastening experience to witness the working sailormen, as he recalls. The *Cambria,* at the end of the Yarmouth tug's towrope, sheered across the harbour in the tide's grip and crushed a small clinker fishing boat moored against the harbour wall.

A woman on a nearby motorboat said: "Ridiculous, bringing a great yacht like that in here." Des said: "I daren't speak to Bob about it until we were out of the harbour, then I said what terrible bad luck it had been. But Bob's reply was, 'That bugger'll buy me a drink on it. Full insurance. He'll be delighted'."

During the passage the eager Des asked to see some charts. Being a stranger to the east coast he wanted to get his bearings.

"Bob was a bit distant, then he directed me to a drawer in his cabin where his shore-going duds were kept. A very ancient chart was lining the bottom. His dog,

Chris Chataway and Bob Roberts aboard *Cambria*.

anyway, slept day-long on a sack over the compass binnacle but Bob didn't have to disturb her. That night at about 3 am and in inky blackness we brought up somewhere on the Whitaker to save a tide. Some hours later when we mustered we had drying sands on three sides of us."

Dusty, Bob's faithful lurcher dog, would curl round the binnacle with her backside to windward. As the barge came about so Dusty would change sides.

Bob's "feel" for where his barge was at any particular time impressed another of his mates, Jimmy Penn. The Everard ship *Annuity* had picked up the *Cambria* in a flat calm off Yarmouth. The *Annuity* was bound for London and had been on passage from Oban. Bob and Jimmy took control of both craft while the crew of the *Annuity* turned in.

"It was thick fog and we motored for hours," said Jimmy. "Bob eventually sent me for'ard with the lead line and we found we had four fathoms. He came out of the wheelhouse and smelt the air, then he asked me to take the wheel. He looked at the compass and said, 'We're just this side of the Blacktail. Give her fifteen fathoms in the water.' I let go and could not see the fifteen fathom mark once it left the hawse, the fog was that thick. Next morning the fog had lifted and the Blacktail Spit buoy was two hundred yards away.

"It was instinct, but Bob shrugged it off with the remark, 'We've got to hit the ground before it hits us'."

Like Harry Bottreill years before, Jimmy also felt humiliated in Bob's gaze after failing to get aloft. They were running up off Aldeburgh one night when it was noticed the spindle holding the bob to the truck had been bent. They reckoned the discharging crane at Yarmouth was responsible. Jimmy shinned up the topsail hoops but on the fifth hoop he slipped and slithered bodily right round the topmast. It put the wind up him and he climbed down.

"Get hold of the wheel," Bob said, and went aloft to do it himself. When he came down on deck he told Jimmy to go and make some tea.

"Make the tea—that was all I was fit for in Bob's eyes."

Jimmy made the tea and brought it on deck. As he lifted his cup he noticed the bob had fouled again. This time he went aloft and actually sat on the topmast truck to free the flag.

"Bob never said one word. In the *Gallon Can* at Yarmouth two weeks later he said, 'Good job you did on that bob'."

Bob had deliberately been harder on Jimmy than he had on Harry. Jimmy had not been recruited from the Erith Yacht Club; he already was a bargeman.

The *Cambria* was no longer a workaday craft unnoticed by the passing world as she carried her freights from the grimy Thames to the east coast ports. She made headlines in local newspapers. The front page of the *Whitstable Times* read "The Last Of The Great Ones—The Barge *Cambria* Attracts Many To Harbour".

In 1956, the *Cambria* attracted the BBC. They wanted the barge to be the vehicle for Olympic runner Chris Chataway's programme contrasting city life with country life. The *Cambria* was to sail round the coast stopping at various places to allow Chris Chataway to step ashore and interview previously briefed rustics. The programme was called *Away From It All*.

During a break in filming Chataway asked Bob if there was a suitable place for him to run. He had been cooped up on board the barge for the sail round to Pin Mill from London. Bob described a seven-mile run round the fields near Dwiny Cottage and, what's more, donned plimsolls to join the champion. Bob was then coming up for fifty with thirteen stones to carry, yet Chataway actually passed the comment, "You're going a bit fast," when Bob sprinted past him on one downhill stretch! In his youth Bob had twice run a marathon for the Cambridge Harriers in the Amateur Athletics Association championships.

On camera Bob could not resist a jibe at Southend as the *Cambria* passed its pier. Asked by Chataway if he would live in a town, he replied, "Not me; too many beer bottles and too much greasy paper flying about." The remark upset the local council's publicity officer, who invited Chataway or Bob to visit Southend's "wooded cliffs, banks of flowers and seclusion"!

On the same programme the old wildfowler Walter Linnett, who once lived in a tumbledown cottage on the marsh side of the sea wall under St Peter's-on-the-wall at Bradwell, produced his own theory on Southend's illuminations and on electric light generally. "I do not think it does anybody any good. A lamp or a candle is far better. You cannot see anything in the dark after electricity. You cannot see any birds. Electricity is killing people's eyes. It is too strong for them."

If the *Cambria* was becoming a novelty to the television viewing public, she was becoming a thorn in the side of London's dockers and lightermen, "dodgers and loitermen" as Bob referred to them.

With her masts and sails the *Cambria* could not be wedged between the ship from which she was to load and the quay without letting go the ship's stern or head ropes. Therefore the dockside crane could not be used and, as a result, the ship's derricks had to be rigged, which made more labour for the stevedores. "Take it back to the museum," was a regular comment from jaundiced dockworkers, or "Where's Nelson, dahn the cabin?" and "Wot, you come 'ere to load cannonballs?"

Once the *Cambria* was loading from a German ship in Tilbury Dock. Two German officers were watching the sacks being lowered down into her hold as

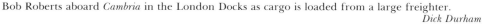

Bob Roberts aboard *Cambria* in the London Docks as cargo is loaded from a large freighter.
Dick Durham

Ron Turner and "Tubs", a docker, with Bob Roberts aboard *Cambria* in the Victoria Docks, London, loading a cargo of peas for Mistley.   *Dick Durham*

they drank tea on the bridge. They spoke good English and were speaking it in a loud voice. Their disparaging remarks raised the hackles of the dockers in the *Cambria's* hold. However much of an anachronism she was to them, it did not mean that foreigners had any right to moan! Eventually one of the officers said as he waved his hand at the *Cambria*, "If that's all England had, how come she won the war?" At this a hook-nosed cockney docker replied in a flash, "If that's all we' ad 'ow come you lost it?"

From those far-off early days aboard the *Garson* at Erith Bob was being invited, sometimes for a fee, to yacht clubs around the east coast to sing and talk about the life he led, the life so many yachtsmen emulated during summer weekends. Unlike the crowd at Erith who simply chuckled when an inebriated Bob fell off the gangplank into the Thames and was kept afloat by his expanded melodeon, other clubs wanted a sterile version of a shellback. Thus, after a thirty-hour voyage from Yarmouth to London, when a weary Bob was driven to the Essex Yacht Club at Leigh-on-Sea for the gentlemen's supper night, his repertoire proved too salty.

His by now good friend Des Sleightholme drove to the Royal Docks to pick him up. It was a dark winter's night and the Port of London Authority (PLA) men at the lock gates had been told the *Cambria* was going to be late on the tide. She was beating up river.

Des said, "Suddenly we saw her out in the stream brailing up. Bob was luffing for the open lock gate under topsail. One of the PLA men said, 'Christ he's going to pile her up.' The *Cambria* came into the circle of the dock gates with nobody on the wheel. Then a voice called up out of the darkness, 'That you up there Des?' I looked down. Bob was calmly pissing over the side, letting the *Cambria* shoot her own way in."

Bob's long haul from Yarmouth had left him tired and hungry but by the time they arrived at the Essex Yacht Club the gentlemen's supper was over. At least, the food had been consumed.

Des said, "They rammed four big scotches down his neck and he went into his act. His songs were so blue that a number of older members walked out. Later we dragged him back to my place; he was singing all the way. He normally gauged his audience and censored his own songs."

Such diplomacy came later when Bob realised what Ernie Sinclair had realised years before—many yacht clubs were merely badged-blazer excuses for social evenings.

At the *Yachts and Yachting* all-male Boat Show dinner the following year Bob received a completely different reaction. Once again the barge was late and Bob arrived straight from the dock dressed in his old serge trousers and navy pullover. He jumped up on stage and announced, "Got a boil on my arse and I've left me teeth back aboard the barge but I'll do my best."

Des commented: "He was a huge success. He was of a breed of seaman-performers, loved an audience, responded to it, yet he was never vain about his talent. On such occasions you saw the real Bob. His gramophone records are no part of him. He was the man who hitched one cheek of his bum on the corner of a pub table, with that toothy grin and those short, square, broken and grimy fingers trailing over the keys of his squeezebox."

Bob Roberts was now irretrievably woven into the fabric of which legends are made. On the river or up the coast, people wanted to greet him, wanted to say hello to Bob Roberts and wanted it to be known that they knew "old Bob". Customs men, dockworkers, tugmen, yachtsmen, all were slightly in awe of Bob and they were baffled by it. What had made him different from the other "characters" thrown up along the London River over the years? What about old Dick Miller? "Dick the Dagger" as he was known lived into his nineties and when asked if he wanted a chair during a barge match said, "When I can't stand up I'll fall down."

Cambria lying at Mistley quay, seen from the quayside maltings, in May, 1970.

The fact is, Bob was the last, literally the last, bargeman and the media liked "pegs". Firsts and lasts and biggests and smallests are the definitives courted by television and newspapers. It was simply publicity that expanded Bob's undoubtedly colourful person into that of a "star".

One night, after a bender ashore, Bob and Des rowed back aboard the *Cambria* in a boat that did not belong to them. They discovered their own boat had been taken and they decided to borrow another. In the morning a passing riverman hailed Bob and informed him he had the police launch boat tied astern. Bob looked aft and sure enough it was. In the distance he could see the bow waves of the police launch heading towards the *Cambria*.

"Bob, badly hungover, only half awake, was nevertheless a match for the occasion," said Des. "He got the first word in. 'Hey officer,' he called across, 'you buggers owe us a pint. We saved your boat last night . . .' "

However Bob was ambivalent about such status. When with journalists and television crews he could not resist playing the macho skipper-entertainer. On the river he played down his contacts with the media and dismissed television people as "actors"—and to Bob actors were "unnecessary" in the order of things.

Once at Ipswich Bob had been drinking with Hervey Benham, the author and pundit on barging matters, and with bargemen. When the pair walked back down to the docks they passed Bob's old office, that of the *East Anglian Daily Times*. Bob stuck his head round the door and said, "Hello, anybody here dead?" There was silence. Bob turned to Hervey and said, "You can't tell," and shut the door again.

Once back afloat nothing could win over the stubborn-minded Ipswich men. Hervey came away back to London that trip. As the *Cambria* came out of the dock there was only a slight draught—a head wind. The *Cambria* turned slowly down river, boxing back and forth as motor barges started coming by. Hervey asked, "Will one give us a little start down, Bob?" "Might, might not," came the gruff reply. Then after a while Bob said, "Go stand on the forehatch. If one sheers across have something ready to chuck them. I doubt if they will."

Hervey said later: "I thought, 'What's the matter with this lot?' as their stern lights passed away below the Cat House. They couldn't see him, they wouldn't see him at all. It was one of my saddest memories."

CHAPTER FIFTEEN

Supplementary Benefit

THE RED SAILS of the *Cambria* would probably not have been sailing so far into the twentieth century if Bob had not earned a supplementary income from his writing and later his broadcasting. Although many bargemen scoffed at his spin-off or rather said disparagingly that it made him a "storybook" sailor, Bob saw to it that others made money out of it as well.

During the early years he had earned cash from his first book *Rough and Tumble* and he made occasional payments to Bully from his royalties.

As his popularity grew with the BBC as a subject for broadcasts he saw to it that others got on the air as well. A good example was a radio broadcast for BBC Midlands Region in 1960. Bob drafted out a rough script for himself and George Dray, the old skipper of the *Greenhithe*. The title was *Storm Force Ten*. George received a fee of six guineas just to read out what Bob had written for him. It was a lively broadcast which included another bargeman, Fred Mackie, as well as the coxswain of the Cromer lifeboat, Henry "Shrimp" Davies, and ship's engineer Harry Bullock.

Bob and George's subject kicked off, strangely enough, with the controversial voyage of the *Greenhithe* which left George a sick man and opened the chance for Bob to take over in his first spritty for Everards'. Bob's footnote to George on the script he had written for him reads: "George—this is only a rough guide. Say it in your own way."

The story is a good one. The *Greenhithe* loads a freight of oil cake from a ship in the Tilbury Dock. George notices how the ship's rails and ladders are smashed, how the deck houses are stove in and how the deck cargo has washed adrift and is strewn everywhere.

He is informed by one of the officers that the ship has sailed through a string of storms since loading oil cake in India. The Indians who loaded the stuff had to be put on an extra twopence a day because they believed the cargo had a voodoo on it.

The *Greenhithe* then inherits this "voodoo". They drag both anchors while brought up in Yarmouth Roads and the *Greenhithe* is beached just clear of Britannia Pier. Relays of horses and carts take the cake out of her at low water and it is found that ninety-two tons of the stuff is unspoilt. The *Greenhithe* is then towed into Yarmouth for repairs. Once off the yard she re-loads the oil cake and sets off again for her destination, Wells in Norfolk. Unfortunately the *Greenhithe* suffers at the hands of another storm, this time from the north-west. She blows all her sails out trying to get back to Yarmouth and drives on to the Scroby Sands. A small motorship manages to get her into Yarmouth where the cargo is discharged.

Bob wrote for George to say: "That cargo never did reach its destination. It was sold in Yarmouth and I was very glad to see the back of it. There was a curse on it when it left India . . . and by the time I got rid of it I'd added a few more."

Back at Pin Mill the net curtains were twitching as "Bob who's been on the wireless" returned. He tried to get his old teacher Percy Quantrill in on the act as well, thinking he would enjoy some extra cash in his retirement.

May Quantrill remembers: "Bob told Percy he could get him on the telly for a few quid, but Percy said he wouldn't have any of it, not if it meant elaborating the truth. Percy said he didn't mind going on telly and telling people how to sail a barge from Pin Mill to London, but he said, 'I'm not going to bloody well lie.' No more was said about it."

In the early sixties Bob again found himself earning money from the world of entertainment, but this time he was joined by another bargeman, Fred Mackie, who now had the *Will Everard*. Both barges, the *Cambria* and the *Will*

The *Greenhithe* is towed through Yarmouth harbour by the steam tug *Richard Lee Barber* in the autumn of 1949. *Tony Farnham collection*

Everard, had been commissioned by a film company and were to report to the St Katharine Dock next to Tower Bridge for the making of *The Amorous Adventures of Moll Flanders*. The barges, they were told, would be converted to "galleons". As Fred saw it, there would be no problem turning the *Cambria* into a period piece but two-inch nails would not be much use for fixing cardboard gunports to the *Will's* steel sides.

Eventually the humble spritties were transformed into the floating stage piece for Moll Flanders, alias Kim Novak, to meet her beloved. Bob, Fred and their respective crews were employed as ship's "minders" and were also on call to move the vessels when required.

At one point in the saga Moll Flanders is in her cabin with her paramour when one ship collides with the other, throwing her through the door. The bargemen had to heave the barges together and as they clashed a yard would fall on deck. It was at this point that the lovely Kim Novak should have crashed through the door, but they could not get a co-ordination which would satisfy the cameramen.

One night, however, it blew a gale and Bob saw his chance. He ordered the *Will Everard* to be hauled upwind from the *Cambria* by about twenty feet. Then, with the film crew's artificial wind and rain machines more than helped by nature's version, they let the *Will* drive down on to the *Cambria*. The *Will* knocked the *Cambria's* galleon stern off and the sailormen thought they would have to start all over again. On the contrary. The filmmakers loved it. Fred said they were given a bottle of rum each and a signed photograph of Kim Novak.

The barges made more money in the five weeks' filming than Mr Will had ever reckoned: £500 a week each.

Fred had grown up the hard way. When a lad he was on the training ship *Arethusa*, an old four-masted barque moored at Lower Upnor on the River Medway. She had been commissioned by the Shaftesbury Homes to prepare "poor boys of good character" for either the Royal Navy or the merchant service. As a result Fred had no romantic notions about sail. When there was no living left to be had in the *Will Everard* he went on to one of Everards' motorships.

The crew of the *Cambria* were delighted when the old barge beat her motorised opposition into port. In 1958 John Haig was mate with Bob and he recalls how the *Cambria* loaded in the London Docks with a clutch of motor-barges. They were all bound for Yarmouth.

"We had a hard slant—it was north-west—and off Harwich all the motor-barges went in and anchored for the night. For us to sail into the harbour meant a dead plug—that was too much like hard work, so we simply carried on.

Cambria discharged in Yarmouth, then the wind veered to the north and blew hard.

"The motor-barges, we later discovered, came out of Harwich to have a look at it but turned back by the time they got to the Ness," John said. "We loaded in

London for Yarmouth again and met the motor-barges coming out of Harwich still loaded with the first freight as we went down the second time!"

On another occasion the *Cambria* was drifting athwart Sea Reach, carried along on the back of a strong spring ebb. She hit Sea Reach No 7 buoy, which John recalls had a cage on it "like a saw". The buoy went beneath the barge and hit the rudder, causing the wheel to spin round so fast that the brass band, which was loosely screwed on, flew off and scarred the roof of the wheelhouse.

She started leaking badly and they had to beach her on the Ray Sand off Leigh-on-Sea. John was then despatched in the barge boat to Southend Pier to ring Everards' for a tug.

"Somebody on the Everard switchboard told the operator reverse charges were reserved for masters and chief engineers. I said: 'Well, say I'm chief engineer of the *Cambria* then', and I think they finally realised it was quite urgent!"

Fred Mackie remembers Bob once making some disparaging though

Cambria towing up to Norwich behind one of the little river tugs in the nineteen-sixties.

The *Cambria* delivering 60 tons of talc at Upnor on the Medway towards the end of 1969. In the background is the training ship *Arethusa*, formerly the *Peking*.   *Dick Durham*

friendly remarks about "motormen" and comparing them with nine till five office workers. "I had words with Bob. I told him, 'When you see those men walking over Tower Bridge wearing their bowler hats and carrying their umbrellas and you think of them as bloody fools, remember they are probably looking down at you pushing and poking the *Cambria* about thinking, 'Look at that bloody fool'."

Yet still there were men who would come for a berth on the *Cambria*. At this time Bob still had a third hand, although John Dickens was the last man to be employed in such a capacity. John shipped aboard straight from school. The only job he had held down previously was a paper round. John helped the mate, Vernon "Vernie" Parker from Colchester, set sail and heave up the anchor. His extra chores were cleaning the brass, blackleading the fireplace, cleaning the oil lamp glasses and trimming the navigation light wicks.

When John was told to tend ropes on deck he soon learned Bob's code of practice with newcomers: "You were allowed two mistakes, and the third time you did it wrong you got a rollicking."

John's initiation was with making a rope fast round a cleat. He led the rope under the cleat instead of over the top and Bob gently corrected him, explaining that by doing it John's way it was likely to jam.

107

"The next time I did it he corrected me a bit more sternly."

Unfortunately John's "third time" was the fault of a passenger. Bob went to ease off the weather vang, found it jammed and skinned his hands trying to clear it.

"He turned to me and said that was a 'blank' thing to do. I felt the other bloke should have owned up but he didn't say a bloody word."

John's first freight was 150 tons of wheat from the King George V Dock to Stambridge Mills up the head of the River Roach. It was almost home again for him, as he lived not far away at Benfleet. At Paglesham, just off the old black weatherboard shed where Frank Shuttlewood built his barges, they engaged a huffler, one of the Keeble family, who turned the barge up the last, winding reaches of the river. The night before, in the *Plough and Sail* at the top of the rutted lane which runs up from the shore, they talked to old Frank. He had a half-model of his dream barge, the barge he would build to beat the famous *Veronica*.

John said: "It was never to be. Sadly, he died soon after of cancer."

During the great freeze in the winter of 1962–63 the *Cambria* lay at Greenhithe loaded with one hundred tons of groundnut cake from Surrey Docks and bound for Yarmouth. The sea was frozen and both Vernie and John went on Everards' yard ashore to make up their lost pay. The *Cambria* eventually made Yarmouth after a five-week delay. She lay stern up the harbour, and when the thaw came a huge "spear" of ice punched a hole in the barge's stern, damage which was not discovered until she went on the ways at Greenhithe. Bob

described it to the occupants of the *White Hart* thus: "We've got an ice-hole up our arse-hole."

John left the *Cambria* and joined an Everards' deep-sea motorship bound for New Zealand. Vernie drifted away.

Phillip "Ginger" Latham was a gangling lad whose boredom with clerical work led him to sign articles as mate of the *Cambria*. He had not been aboard many months when the barge was blown across to Dunkirk in a north-westerly storm. She had left Yarmouth on 29th November, 1962, arrived in Dunkirk the following day, having lost her mainsail, arrived back at Greenhithe on 18th December, after the racing barge *Sara's* mainsail had been sent across by a rival company's motorship, and was back in Yarmouth with 150 tons of groundnut cake by 23rd December.

In just under one month Ginger's skinny frame had thickened into that of a muscular sailor.

In 1963 Bob's old racing barge the *Dreadnought* was broken up and burnt at Everards' yard. The company had decided it was time to end their association

Right: Bob Roberts had charge of the *Dreadnought* in the races from 1958 onwards, but she was broken up at Greenhithe in 1963.
Tony Farnham collection

Opposite: Breaking up the *Sara* at Greenhithe. Everards' decided to break her up rather than let her fall into the hands of amateur sailors.

109

Cambria off Gravesend in 1963. She is making the best of a smart breeze and still wears Everards'
bob; within three years the firm had sold her to her master.   *Tony Farnham collection*

with sail. Two years later they disposed of all their sailing fleet. The *Sara* was
broken up rather than left to the hands of amateur racing enthusiasts, the *Will
Everard* was disposed of, the *Veronica* was sold for a houseboat. The only sailing
vessel left in the fleet was the *Cambria*, and her future looked grim.

There was plenty of outrage at the "vandalism" by Everards'. Bob supported
the company. He agreed that the barges should not go to novices, but his old
friend Hervey Benham did not.

"It was bloody-mindedness. And I blame King George V. When he said that
bloody amateurs weren't going to lay their fingers on his yacht and instead he
had the *Britannia* burnt, I remember thinking, 'You vulgar old bastard, I'll
become a republican. Why the hell shouldn't somebody else sail your effing
boat? The taxpayers paid for it'." The taxpayers had not paid for the *Veronica* or
the *Sara*, of course, but Hervey added: "It was the Everard outlook, having to
smash them up rather than let them be used as yacht-barges."

Bert Fry remembers the Everard outlook: "Miss Ethel was quite straight
about it. She said, 'I'm not interested in barges.' There was no sentimentality in
them."

110

Even Ginger sympathised with the old firm: "They were surviving in a very competitive world and wished to sever the link with sailing barges as they were no longer necessary, no longer advantageous in publicity or economically justifiable. Bob and I may have had other views but it wasn't our money. They were a paternalistic company demanding acquiescence, in return for which they looked after their own. Bob's attitude in refusing to take a modern motorship commanded respect at first but finally no great love."

On 2nd February, 1966, Bob Roberts, by special arrangement, bought from Everards' the last sailing vessel to trade under the red ensign, the *Cambria*.

That year he earned quite well from the barge. She carried one extra freight over 1965's total of sixteen cargoes. Also, yet again, the *Cambria* was contracted by the BBC. However, if Bob had known what the televised result would turn out to be, he would never have let the cameras aboard. He was led to believe that the Corporation was interested in making a non-fiction documentary on the last sailing barge. A freelance producer named Colin Morris shipped aboard for a trip from Pin Mill to London.

By the time filming was ready to start it had been discovered that instead of a documentary a soap opera based on Bob Roberts was to be made under the title *King of the River*. The title came from the hero's name, Jos King, played, much to Bob's dismay, by the actor Bernard Lee. During part of the filming John Dickens sailed in Ginger's place while Ginger took a holiday. John recalls: "Lee was an overweight, gutty sort of guy, Bob called him "Blubberguts", and felt a bit insulted that Bernard Lee had been chosen to portray him. I don't think I would have been too happy myself."

In one episode Jos King was supposed to race and beat a motor-barge. This was filmed off Sheerness.

John said: "In practice the motor-barge *Convoy* towed us as it was a flat calm. Lee would be at the wheel but he had difficulty remembering his lines and the guy that played the mate didn't come across very well either. He was small and very slight. Captain Birdseye would have been better than him. The pair of them weren't very convincing." In one scene Mr Lee had to row the barge's boat. However he could not manipulate oars. John hid beneath canvas in the bilges while the actor attempted a few strokes under the camera's gaze, then John would come out of hiding and row him back into position.

Bernard Lee got off to a bad start with Bob by barging into the cabin without knocking. Bob asked him if he behaved like that at home and from then on things deteriorated. The actor was overheard boasting to his film crew that he could take Bob on in a bare-knuckle fight with one hand tied behind his back. Bob's reply was to invite him to meet him on the hatches—with both hands free.

"Mr Lee displayed some intelligence by refusing, and was ordered off the barge," John recalled.

Bob was eventually talked round by the director and the filming was finished, but a thin dialogue and further eruptions caused the whole crew to lose heart with their marine soap opera and to kill it off. The scriptwriters relocated Mr Lee as a shore-based, retired barge skipper who delivered yachts! Bob was still fuming, however, and he complained to the then head of BBC 2, David Attenborough. David had been on the barge for a trip some years before.

The critics did not think much of the television serial. James Thomas in the *Daily Express* wrote: "Here is Bernard Lee as the last skipper of a sailing barge on the Thames, harbouring a runaway Russian sailor, fighting for an efficient life-boat crew, sparring with a tough blonde publican and trying to keep a kooky daughter from running away to sea. In fifty minutes enough characters were

Bob Roberts at the wheel of *Cambria*. This photograph was used for publicity purposes when Bob told stories of the sea in the children's television programme *Jackanory*. *BBC photograph*

established to staff *Crossroads* [a now defunct television soap opera] for three months. Inevitably there was a sad, dramatic emptiness . . ."

He should have been aboard.

Hervey Benham made some passages aboard the barge and admired Bob's calm control as he brought her about. "He had the most impressive thought communication, a very quiet sort of 'Oh, oh, we're coming round . . . oh-oh that'll do'."

Hervey was irritated by Bob's stance on non-professional bargemen. One of his daughter's friends was rigging out the *Thalatta* for charter work and Hervey would have preferred it if Bob had given his blessing to the growing movement of re-rigging barges for yachts. Consequently Hervey picked out the hypocrisies, as he saw them, in Bob's life. He told him: "You do the red sails in the sunset bit and then go off to Lime Grove."

Bob's reply satisfied the gnarled author: "If I could do barging only I'd do barging only. But Anne's art school fees aren't part of barging, so I've got to do something outside of the barging world to pay for it."

One voyage for which Bob had become quite famous was a trip to Yarmouth when there was very little wind. He got the crew to row a kedge out ahead of the barge, drop it, then repeat the process to make a laborious snail's progress. Such devotion to making the passage caused Hervey to comment, "Once you've got ink in your blood, as Bob had, you're already subconsciously writing the story before you do the thing and then you've got to create the material for the story.

"Why didn't Bob take the logical progression and go into a six-hundred-ton motorship? The answer is, he got hooked on his own bait. There was a genuine touch of the creative romantic in him. He was a product of the times."

Bob was certainly not shy about being creative in his business affairs. In February, 1967, the *Cambria* was damaged when the tug *Spartan* clouted her in the London River. Part of his damage report to The Shipowners' Protection and Indemnity Association Ltd reads: "Other lightermen present, with their well-known enthusiasm for work and efficiency, were completely apathetic when asked if they would be witness and shrugged their shoulders (this can be done without taking the hands out of the pockets) and commented that they 'don't want to know' . . ."

Many people got the chance to experience the last sailing ship as Bob rarely refused anyone a berth if they were interested. Some were spellbound with the simplest predicament. One such was a yachtsman from Erith Yacht Club who whispered under his breath as he watched the *Cambria* grip to her anchor under the shelter of the half-tide sands of the Buxey one night, "Coo, just like in the books." Bob's books, presumably.

Others had pretty unnerving experiences. One of the worst happened to Ron Turner, a superintendent with London's river police. The *Cambria* had brought up on the edge of Yantlet Flats at the end of the ebb tide one night on her way to Mistley. Ron had turned in and was fast asleep in the fo'c'sle.

"Suddenly there was the blast of a ship's siren. There was no time lapse between bunk and forecastle head. I stood on deck looking aft and saw Bob looking forward, we were both dressed only in singlet and pants.

"Towering over us, very close to, was this thirty thousand ton bulk carrier heeling over to starboard as she sheered away from us with white faces of disbelief staring down at us in awe that we had not been run down."

They later discovered a half hitch of chain had dropped over one anchor fluke. As the flood tide lifted the barge, the knot closed around the anchor, plucked it from the mud and, trailing the bight of paid out chain, the *Cambria* had drifted into the shipping lanes. Ron had set the anchor light wick too low and the glass had smoked up. The ship probably registered a small blip on her radar but could not see the barge until it was almost too late. A Port of London Authority launch arrived to investigate, and the officers were satisfied with Bob's explanation, strange as it was. Bob himself told Ron he had only once before ever heard of a barge picking up her anchor in such a fashion.

Bob was later invited as guest speaker to the Thames Police Association annual dinner aboard *HMS President* alongside the Victoria Embankment. His final words signalled the end of the *Cambria's* days. With some emotion he told those gathered: "I, being the last of the commercial sailormen, wish to thank on behalf of myself and all those sailormen who have gone before me, you men of the river who have helped, assisted and never persecuted. No matter what hour, day or year whenever we have needed you, you have been there.

"In the passing of my kind so will your history change."

Cambria in the River Roach at Paglesham with 150 tons of wheat for Stambridge Mills, June, 1970.

CHAPTER SIXTEEN

Life on Board

EVEN the dialling tone of Woolverstone 253 sounded like a thing of the past. I listened to the faint, leisurely purring noise and wondered if it belonged to a sit-up-and-beg style telephone with a dusty plaited cord . . . click. A soft, refined voice told me it was Mrs Roberts speaking.

Yes, her husband had received my letter. He had indeed received several applying for the job as mate of the *Cambria* but he was windbound in Flushing, Holland, at the moment. Tony told me they had sailed across there in Jerry Thomason's yacht *Chica* while the *Cambria* lay on Pin Mill hard for summer repairs. Tony had fallen and broken a rib, and had returned to Harwich by ferry.

"He's stuck in Holland with these westerly winds," she told me, "but I've got a message for you. He says keep your eye out of window and when the wind turns north-east wait a couple of days and come up."

Thus my interview date was fixed.

It was September, 1969, and the wind did veer to the north-east some days later. I gave it a forty-eight hour spell, then arrived in Pin Mill. Bob had not long been home. He appeared to my seventeen-year-old eyes at first sight less formidable than I had expected. Quite what I had expected I am not sure but he was friendly, if distant, and very businesslike. I was told to go down to the hard and look at the barge while Bob finished entertaining friends who had been with him in Flushing. It turned out that one of them, Sheila Blackburn, had been spared from the second yacht *Lilly Bolero* to help Bob sail home.

The *Cambria's* massive grey bows dominated all other craft on the pebble hard. Heavy clinker-built skiffs lay canted this way and that down either side of the *Cambria's* flanks, as though she had cleaved her way through all the clutter of yachts with the privilege of commerce. Her thirty-two-foot bowsprit hung threateningly over the heads of the villagers. She seemed so big sitting there for her overhaul. I climbed a paint-spattered ladder and stood on deck. On the hatches were coils of huge ropes resembling sleeping boa constrictors. I looked aloft at the maze of running rigging, trying to follow the various lines from winch to clew or tack, and I began to wonder if I had taken on a job which I could not do. Sailing eighteen-footers was all right but this was different altogether. I had just decided to refuse the job politely if it were offered when Bob climbed over the rail. He asked me a few questions and then, before I had time to let him know I was wasting his time, he said, "Well, you seem suitable enough to me. Come over next weekend and paint out the fo'c'sle. I'll start you on wages from then."

I was simply too timid to tell Bob of my doubts after his breezy, direct appointment and thus I became mate of the *Cambria*.

The following weekend I waited outside the *Butt and Oyster* in the early morning for the tide to ebb away from the *Cambria*, then I waded out to the ladder in my thighboots. Reuben Webb, a local shipwright, was offering up a piece of timber to a hole in the covering board.

"You the noo mate?" he asked.

"Yes", I replied proudly.

"You won't earn nuthin' here. These is done for," he said.

It did not matter to me. I had broken the indentures I had signed to work for a small building firm. As an apprentice "construction technician" I had learned a lot about picking up broken bricks and removing them from one pile to another. During my long and dreary days at the wheel of the cement-mixer I had dreamed that I was at the helm of a barge. The last thing I wanted was a future. To me, a future had been a four-year agreement to labour cheaply for a builder in return for a qualification and a chance of joining the pension scheme.

In early September we sailed for Grays with Peter Sharman aboard to show me the ropes.

One of the first lessons I learned about the barge was that you do not stand in the way of the wind. The helmsman needs to feel the wind on his face, especially at night, "so's he knows how close he is steering to it". Several times I stood listening intently to Bob's stories as he steered, but I stood to windward, between him and the wind. To correct the error of my ways and to teach me to stand to "loo'ard" Bob ran round in front of me and stamped on my feet with the wooden clogs he always wore aboard.

It was during our second freight I learned of the old man's intolerance with crews who showed no spunk aloft. We were bound for Fingringhoe with 150 tons of wheat, coming in from the Spitway, shaping up for the Colne. Bob asked me to clear the topsail tack which had fouled the mainmast cap. At the crosstrees, having reached the end of the ratlines and thus easy climbing, I wondered how I would get up further. It seemed impossible. I shouted down to Bob, "I don't think I can get up any further."

He left the wheel and walked to the rail, clearly composing his reply. He looked under the mainsail and, having satisfied himself all was clear to leeward, he walked back to the wheel, looked up at me and said, "Well, I've been up there and I'm sixty. How old are you?" I was seventeen and I got the point. I reached

Wearing Bob Roberts' own bob, the *Cambria* makes a board across the Thames at Woolwich.   *BBC photograph*

the mainmast cap, cleared the sail, then wondered if it was safe to come down!

Something many people recognised in Bob was his ability to get others to realise their potential. Two months after this episode I was sitting on the topmast truck erecting the new "flying seagulls" bob which was the master's personal houseflag.

However, one circus act I could never master was hand-over-handing up the vangs. The topsail sheet parted once as the *Cambria* was bound up off the Naze. Bob ordered me forward to drop the halyard. The whole rig was shuddering from the uncontrolled topsail yanking at the mast. Once the sail was down I tried to climb the vangs to retrieve the bitter end. I failed. Later, on Grays' buoy, I climbed along the mainsail headrope and brought it down that way.

Bob was unimpressed. He described it as "the piss-artist's route", an oblique reference to an earlier little *contretemps* we'd had. *Cambria* was laid up at Grays for a two-month overhaul. We lowered the rig down and Bob went off on holiday while I agreed to stay aboard painting, taking the weekends off to go home to Leigh. In those two weeks I painted the entire barge from chine to rail capping outside and from ceiling to hatch coaming inside. Bob returned on the second Friday while I was lunching in the *Theobalds Arms*. I spotted him scraping at one end of the sprit. Mildly surprised that he had not come into the pub, I nevertheless sprang aboard, looking forward to a praiseworthy remark about my hard work. Without looking up Bob muttered: "We won't get this job done in the pub." I was so incensed I put sixty-six feet of pitch-pine between us and started work at the other end of the sprit!

Opposite: Bob Roberts, Penny the collie and the author on board *Cambria* at Colchester Hythe after delivering 100 tons of groundnut cake in February, 1970. *Colchester Express*

Right: Bob Roberts and the author scraping *Cambria's* topmast at Grays in March, 1970. *Dick Durham*

Back in the late fifties a tough bullet-headed young man came all the way from Australia simply to ask Bob to teach him to sail. Bill Nance immediately impressed Bob. He was a hard-bitten loner who had lost the tops of several fingers in a mining accident back home and had consequently had steel finger-tips fitted as a replacement. He was also well read, and he soon became a successful mate of the *Cambria*. Having learnt to sail he bought a yacht, the *Cardinal Vertue*, and sailed her back to Aussie, only to arrive at Fremantle and be told he would have to pay import duty on the yacht.

Sheila remembers Bob's delight at the letter Bill eventually sent him from New Zealand. "Bill had been allowed ashore at Fremantle to buy a loaf of bread. Then, refusing to pay the duty, he sailed on to Auckland and sold the boat there!"

Bob's hard attitude was based on his idea of what a seaman should be like. He would often tell with some glee the apocryphal stories surrounding the spartan bargemasters of long ago. One was about the old skipper who was aghast when he spotted his mate spreading margarine and jam on his bread. Bob would mimic this long-forgotten sailor's squawky voice. "Bread and marge, boy, or bread and jam but not bread, marge and jam."

Food aboard the *Cambria* was usually plentiful but sometimes it would run low. I remember once, when we had run short of food and had spent a couple of days eating potatoes and little else, I discovered some lamb's liver on a plate in one of the saloon lockers and eagerly told Bob. Quite dispassionately he informed me it was for Penny, the border collie that sailed with us!

After taking our turns at breakfast—the other would be at the wheel—I would go down to make coffee. During the winter months I would still be hungry but felt guilty taking any more from the loaf. As the man at the helm could hear all the noises being made in the saloon below I used to cough loudly to cover the sound of the breadknife sawing through an extra couple of slices.

Invariably Bob would use the scissors from the *Cambria's* medical kit to cut up Penny's dinner. The medical manual kept in the saloon was almost pornographic with its lurid coloured photographs of the disgusting things apparently picked up exclusively by sailors. I had nightmare visions of Bob craning over my prostrate body on the hatches, the wind blowing the pages of the manual over as he wiped the medical scissors clean to make the first incision to remove my diseased appendix. Jimmy Penn once underwent "surgery" at Bob's hand. A sprig of rusty wire stabbed his arm and the wound turned septic. Bob told him it would have to be lanced, and proceeded to boil up some water in a saucepan. Then, aided by a piece of lint, Germolene and a sailmaker's needle sterilised in the saucepan, Bob held Jimmy in a half-Nelson and "squashed the poison right down my arm," in Jimmy's pictorial words.

The first time I dropped the foresail I almost became a hospital case myself. Having lifted the pawl on the halyard winch I left the handle on the spindle and let it fly. The heavy cast iron handle flew round like a propeller. Bob shouted to me to stand clear and later explained it was more prudent to grab hold of the halyard, take the handle off and then let go of the halyard.

Lessons were learned the hard way. Sometimes I mistook his orders. His

The author at the wheel of *Cambria.*   *Dick Durham*

120

gruff voice garbled tops'l when he meant foresail, or so it sounded to me. If I dropped the wrong sail it was me who had to heave it up again. Another time we were sailing up Sea Reach when I was at the wheel. Bob was walking around the deck coiling down ropes when he suddenly turned to me and said, "Starboard your helm," as he rolled his hands to port. Stupidly I put the helm to port. I should have been guided by his verbal command not his gesticulations. We hit a boat crawling with anglers. They made various remarks about blindness but Bob was quickly on the defensive. He told them in no uncertain terms what happened to craft that anchored in the fairway, even though they were just on the edge of the Shoebury sand for the fish (however, on the channel side of the marker buoys), and we were just on the edge of it to keep out of the ebb tide.

Those patient men who sit for hours dipping their hooks were graded below yachtsmen in the sailormen's list of pests.

One dark night we were sailing up the Wallet bound for London. All looked clear ahead when suddenly a light came on, wavered, and went out. Bob sent me for'ard to keep a look-out. As I walked along the deck I was astonished to see a small dinghy with a cabin about twice the size of the hull bobbing by just a few feet from the leeboard. In the stern sat two anglers innocently munching sandwiches. Then one of them switched on a torch, baited his hook, dropped his tackle over the side and switched out his light. Before the darkness swallowed them up again one of them completed the blissful ignorance of their position; he waved. The *Cambria* could have sent two bounteous pieces of bait for the crabs that night and no one would ever have known.

It was left to old George Burroughes, as usual, to classify the breed with nutshell precision. "An angler, booee, you know what that is, don't you? That's a bit of line with a wahm on one end and a bloody fooell on the other."

Bob's wrath towards anyone or anything that jeopardised the correct running of the barge did not discriminate between right and wrong.

Once the *Cambria* had spent a week laying at Grays waiting for orders. Bob had driven to Lowestoft to pick up our life raft which had undergone a Board of Trade survey, and we had arranged to meet in the *Theobalds Arms* the following Monday lunchtime.

Closing time arrived and still Bob had not shown up. I went home by train to Leigh, intending to be in the pub the following lunchtime. Little did I know that Bob had already telephoned the agent, Sully, and received orders to load one hundred tons of cattle cake in the Royal Albert Dock. The ship would be ready for us on Tuesday afternoon. I should have stayed aboard but thought we would again be fobbed off with "ring tomorrow for orders" as we had been for days on end.

At breakfast time on Tuesday morning Bob rang me at home. His blistering message ended with, "So you'd better get up here as quick as ever you can."

We were under way by 10 am. High water was at 1 pm. The wind was

121

westerly, moderate. Bob said: "We needed a whole tide to make the Gallions entrance with the wind in this quarter".

In Halfway Reach we mis-fetched and narrowly missed colliding with a fast moving freighter. We were pinching the *Cambria* over the ebb, an ebb, were it not for me, we would not have encountered. We had to bring up just under Ford's huge factory.

It seemed to me that any misfortune which befell us now would be my fault. It was my error which had sealed the fate of the *Cambria's* passage. After a hostile meal aft, Bob nodded off on the locker and I slunk away for'ard to read in order to take my mind off things. Times were hard enough as it was, I thought as I lay

Bob Roberts out on the *Cambria's* bowsprit furling the jib.   *Roger Finch*

miserably in my bunk. Bob told me he earned about £17 a week after he had paid for everything. I was on £5 a week. Freights were hard enough to get without throwing them away by negligence. Eventually slack water came and we got under way again.

We arrived at the Gallions entrance. As usual I had to walk along to the lock master's hut to wake up the guardian of what was once one of the world's busiest docks in order that he could let us in. Men shuffled out in the darkness. "What craft are yer?" said one. Then noticing our masts, another said, "Gawd, take it away. Makes me feel seasick." The last thing I felt like hearing was any "funnies" from our Port of London Authority friends but I was overjoyed to hear that our ship, the *Loch Ryan*, had not yet arrived and was not due in until the following morning. Bob became distinctly warmer. He was never a man to harbour bad feelings.

However, the mate could feel the whiplash of Bob's tongue even if he was not in the wrong. Once we took another one hundred tons of peas from the Royal Victoria Dock to Mistley on the River Stour in Essex.

We beat up the river and just got a turn on the motor-barge *Raybel* before the ebb came away. Bob and I were on the bowsprit stowing the jib when the barge started swinging out from the *Raybel*, as her head was levered away by the wash. I raced along the bowsprit and shouted at the mate of the *Raybel* who had taken our for'ard breastrope and failed to make it fast properly. He saw what was happening and tried to make up some extra turns but it was too late. I threw him another rope but by this time the *Cambria* had swung through ninety degrees and her bows had touched the far bank of the creek.

Bob yelled at me to take a line from her starboard bow in the boat and make it fast ashore with the idea of pulling her right round 180 degrees so that she was facing down river. He was understandably worried that the *Cambria* would break her back on the falling tide as the grounded bow left the hull amidships unsupported. As I fumbled with the rope, while trying to scull the boat at the same time, Bob shouted all sorts of abuse, mainly founded on the observation that Penny could do a better job than could I!

We fortunately got a line ashore and heaved the *Cambria's* head clear of the bank on the dolly winch. Bob chastised me. He said I should have checked not only the turn I had made but the one on the other barge as well.

On another occasion the *Cambria* broke her anchor out on the wrong tack as we were getting under way in the Colne. She fell alongside the wreck which lies just off East Mersea. A little motorboat put out from Brightlingsea and started negotiations to tow us off. He asked for £5 but Bob said he only had £3 aboard. Foolishly I said I had got £5 in the fo'c'sle. From Bob's weary expression I could tell I had a long way to go in learning how to survive as a sailorman in 1970.

Sharp practice aboard eked out our meagre earnings. We acquired coal from lighters in the London River and other odd locations. I once spent the

evening filling the coal lockers aft from the furnaces of the Mistley maltings, only to discover it was some rock hard anthracite that would not burn on a domestic fire.

There had been many longshoremen who had scratched a living from the traffic of the Thames. One such was Fred Lapslie, who had for a time been mate in the *Cambria* between hovering around the Erith saltings breaking ancient yachts for their lead keels. His most celebrated "touch" was an order to make a laying-up cover for a large yacht bound round to the Solent and owned by a

Opposite: Towing out of the Royal Albert Dock with a cargo of fishmeal for Great Yarmouth.
Tony Farnham collection

Right: Fred Lapslie, one-time mate of the *Cambria*.

distinguished lady barrister. The cover was delivered, the yacht went away and Fred thought that was the last he would see of it and the lady barrister. Many years later Fred was summoned for jury service. As he sat fidgeting in court he slowly began to recognise the defence counsel. At the end of the case Fred shuffled hurriedly out of the building but the lady barrister headed him off with the chastening remark: "It's Mr Lapslie isn't it? Thank you for the excellent cover. I wonder if next time you could supply me one without William Cory and Son emblazoned on the side?"

It seemed the yachtsman would be the victim whether in town or country. Bob and I once visited a pub called the *Ship* in the village of Levington on the opposite side of the River Orwell to Pin Mill.

We entered at opening time. The little bare-floorboarded bar with its pew-style seats and ticking clock was empty. Behind the bar red flagstones led to

125

a latched door, from the other side of which we could hear the sounds of wood being chopped. When the landlord was ready to serve us he came out silently. We made various observations on the area, trying to draw the old man out, but he remained tight-lipped until I said, "You're very near the river here. You must get a lot of yachtsmen coming in here in the summer."

The old man looked me full in the face and replied, "Yes, get a lot of yachtsmen coming in here in the summer. They come in here and asks for a pint of best. Well I ain't got no best here, it's all one brew, so if they asks for a pint of best I just charges them thruppence more."

Down the road from the pub and across the river we could see the *Cambria's* distinctive and now unique outline—the two sides of a triangle formed by masts and sprit. Her silhouette fused into the elms on the bank behind her as the twilight dwindled. Later as we passed the pub I overheard someone point Bob out to his companion saying, "He's the last one."

I laughed over the remark with Bob, who said, "Perhaps they'll have me stuffed for the Natural History Museum."

One dark winter's night we could not save our tide through the Spitway, a submerged swatch running through the Gunfleet Sands, and the wind was against us. Bob shouted at me through the dark. "We'll bring up under the Buxey. It'll give us a bit of shelter. We'll have one last board before we bring up." We made the board but then I could hear Bob bawling at me to come aft. Earlier I had taken in the mainsheet a few inches. I had not noticed that the mainsheet block pin was poking between the leeboard pendant wires and I had therefore

lashed the wire to the block. As the *Cambria* winded she pulled up the weather leeboard automatically by stretching the wire tight across the deck as the mainsheet traveller thwacked across. We went about again and I cleared the wire. Bob said: "Your job as mate is to make sure everything runs freely and that nothing gets foul."

On another occasion I fell asleep at the wheel while the *Cambria* was running down Swin off the Blacktail Spit. It was virtually a flat calm, fortunately, for the barge gybed all standing, bringing Bob up from his bunk. "Don't do that again lad. You'll have the effing lot out of her."

After that it did not take any black coffee to keep me awake.

Once entering Felixstowe I needed neither coffee nor matchsticks to keep my eyes open. The entrance there is narrow and the dock itself is small. We needed to keep almost all sail on the barge so that she would not sag off to leeward on the ebb and miss it. As Bob rounded her up and steered for the entrance I stood on the mast deck and nervously hoped that I would not make a bungle or be too slow at getting the sail off her when the time came. As we neared the entrance I noticed a crowd had gathered near the dock and were watching us. They made me feel even more self-conscious. "Come on Bob," I thought as we got closer, "tell me to pick up the mainsail." He said nothing. I turned and looked aft with a pleading look on my face. He was not looking at me but was carefully judging our leeway.

"It's no good, she won't make it this time," he yelled and then added, "Stand by yer bowlin'." He spun the wheel to port and we came about. The *Cambria*

Opposite: *Cambria* lying at the Clamp after taking 160 tons of wheat from Tilbury Terminal to Felixstowe Dock.

Right: The barges *Cambria* and *Will Everard* alongside the motor coaster *Asperity* at Greenhithe. In the background can be seen the training ship *Worcester*.
Tony Farnham collection

came round, lifting up and down on the swell like a swingboat. The wheelhouse was dwarfed by the entrance jetty. I could have counted the pile bolts, we were that close.

Once again we nosed towards the entrance. A young mother turned her pram round to allow her baby a view. I envied that little babe as we neared and would gladly have changed places . . .

"Right oh, pick up your mains'l" shouted Bob.

With a parched throat and shaking arms I fumbled the handle on to the brails winch. Once it was on I wound like a madman and leapt back and forth from the winch to heave in on the middle and lower brails as well. I had only just got a second turn on the cleat when Bob said, "Down tops'l," and, immediately afterwards, "Down stays'l." I jumped about the deck as though it was the lid of a furnace. It was not until I had dropped both sails I realised we were in. The pram was turned again as we raced past the crowd to the far side of the harbour. Again I looked aft expectantly at Bob and he yelled, "Stand by your anchor," and then, "Leggo!"

Frantically I tore at the turns of chain and threw them round the splintery barrel. By now I was feeling very pleased with myself and looked back to the admiring faces of our audience. Then I chucked the second turn of the chain over the first and, as the anchor pulled out the slack, the heavy links ground together in a little cloud of rust, jamming the windlass solid.

"All right mate?" asked Bob as he nipped for'ard to see how she checked. He saw my face gaping at the rapidly approaching harbour wall and then noticed the chain. "You bloody idiot," he said, but then the *Cambria* slowed, stopped and began to swing. Mercifully, enough slack had clanked away to enable the anchor to grip the harbour floor before I had jammed the windlass.

Bob gave me a quiet fore deck lecture and all was forgotten. When the time came to leave Felixstowe the wind was blowing force nine to ten. We had no choice but to leave as there was no room in the dock and another ship wanted our berth. We anchored in Harwich Harbour, the weather being too foul to leave. That night, even with twenty fathoms, the *Cambria* started dragging. My torch showed Bob's great hand on the chain waiting for the telltale rumble.

Later I asked Bob what we would have done had the barge dragged ashore. "Caught the bus home," came his droll reply.

In all earnest, Bob was becoming increasingly aware of his age. With no son to help him, as only a son could be expected to help, Bob had morbid thoughts about death. He told me about an elderly boatbuilder in Suffolk whose wife would help him in his yard, holding up the timbers while he fixed them. They, too, had no family. When the old man became too weak to lift the timbers any more he slit this throat with a chisel rather than, as Bob put it, "lie down and die a cow's death". An old bargeman who was himself dying told Bob the story.

CHAPTER SEVENTEEN

Grays for Orders

NOWHERE on the London River was the *Cambria's* stem rubbed more thoroughly into 1970 than at the Tilbury Grain Terminal. This fully automated cereal dispensing leviathan almost sank the barge on one of her early visits there.

We had orders to load 150 tons of maize for Fingringhoe. At close to low water the *Cambria* had just surged back on her mooring springs when a huge steel pipe snaked down at us from somewhere far above, accompanied by a cacophony of discordant bells. Fortunately we had uncovered the barge, for no sooner had the pipe articulated itself into the "firing" position than forty-five tons of maize roared out in ten minutes. The grain shot into the starboard quarter and the *Cambria* dipped over alarmingly. I could see the black bilge water splash up the lining of the hold out on to the maize, only to be immediately covered with more grain.

Bob frantically shouted up at this faceless array of technology. Miraculously a human face appeared about forty feet overhead, but wearing his safety helmet and ear-protectors the owner of the face could not understand Bob's anxious orders to move the pipe amidships and to the middle of the hold. Presumably this little humanoid, connected to his spewing giant by a hand control box, recognised that the barge had described an unusual elevation, and the pipe, which did not stop disgorging maize, was moved.

On shore the massive white silos, full with grain, loomed through the dust like the towers of some grotesque castle. We could tend to nothing else. All that mattered was getting the crude vomiting snake moved in equal measure about the hold. Bells announced its descent, buzzers the onset of grain. Twenty-five minutes later the *Cambria* was loaded with 150 tons of maize, before the slowly falling dust had settled on her decks.

When Bill Everard chose the grown oak trees from the small forest behind Greenhithe to build his barge he had not reckoned on a load of four and a half tons per minute!

The grain snake's deluge slowed to a trickle, there was a rattle and then it receded, folding up and away into itself as the tiny click of metallic voice screamed, "*Cambria* make your berth clear, make your berth clear." We hauled the barge out of the berth across to a road of lighters and covered up. The grey and shrunken boards of the mill at Fingringhoe could not have provided a better contrast had Hollywood scripted it. At the head of a tortuous creek the hour or so of tide ebbed and deposited the *Cambria's* old timbers snugly into the ooze.

A weekend drifted by, with strolls to the nearby *Whalebone Inn*. On Monday morning old Jock arrived in his pullover and I made him a mug of tea. He helped me to uncover, then he swung out a rusty tube on a creaking derrick and lowered it into the "maizes" as he plurally described them. A little hole appeared in our freight. Very slowly the hole got bigger and an hour later the *Cambria* was ten tons lighter.

Two days later Jock got round to taking off his pullover and donning overalls. By now the hole was big enough for him to climb down and shovel the last of the maize towards the suction tube.

Commerce in the London docks was also conducted at a leisurely pace, but for different reasons. The *Cambria* was, simply, hard work for the dockers. With her wide coaster's decks they had to "wing out" the bags of cargo, which meant lifting each bag individually from the "set" of bags dropped into the centre of the hold by dock crane or ship's derrick and re-stowing it up against the side. They would take care of a few sets, then rapidly get bored with the task and "draw" the strops—get the crane to lift the strop out, tumbling the bags over any old how. Bad stowage in a sailing ship is a hazard. Later at sea the cargo can shift, giving

Left: Old Jock enjoying a mug of tea as 150 tons of maize, loaded at Tilbury Terminal in 25 minutes, is sucked out at Fingringhoe mill at the rate of 10 tons an hour.
Dick Durham

Opposite: An example of London stowage—100 tons of cattle cake loaded in Tilbury Dock for Mistley. *Dick Durham*

the vessel a fatal list. This meant that Bob and I had to get down with the dockers and do their work for them.

The *Cambria* could load 150 tons of bagged cargo below decks. When we had orders for 122 tons of maize starch from the Royal Albert Dock to Otterham in Kent, we watched the sacks creeping up to the deckhead, before we were half loaded, with gloom. Although either Bob or I kept a tally of the cargo going in and out, if there was a fiddle being worked there was little we could do for fear of being blacked. Dealing with these subtleties was all part of what Bob described as "dockology". On this particular freight it is not hard to imagine Bob's fury when, already in the knowledge that we were going to have to carry a stack, he was informed the *Cambria* had loaded only one hundred tons; Bob had already tallied in our full freight. He refused to be fobbed off with the extra, the result of some intrigue or simple careless accounting. It became clear that the ship worker had made a mistake when he eventually admitted we had a full freight and asked us to take the extra. "You can flog it the other end," he said encouragingly. Bob later said it had not been worth refusing. Times were hard enough for the barge as things were and it was only a river freight. We sailed to Otterham with a nine-bag stack on the main hold and two on the forehold.

It was the *Cambria's* last freight from the Royal Docks. We nipped our boat

in the lock and had to haul it up in the davits. It was close to low water and the barge was low in the lock when one of the Port of London Authority hands helpfully dropped the retrieved thwarts from our sunken boat on to the stack, reducing them to matchwood. With the depressing sound of water trickling out of the split planks and a tear in our hatch cloth we towed out into the river behind a flotilla of lighters. As we slipped off our turn the lock hands unwittingly watched the last sailorman shape away down river.

While the *Cambria* could be lumbered with too much freight she was more often rooked of her true ration. We had orders to load one hundred tons of peas from a ship in the Royal Victoria Dock for Mistley. With us was the motor barge *Beatrice Maud* whose skipper, Harold Smy, also had one hundred tons to load "ex-ss *Dinteldyke*". Harold, who saw himself as an authority on "sailorising" and in later years was to advise Egyptian mariners on how to caulk their dhows during a holiday to the Nile with his wife, loaded first. By the time the *Cambria* got alongside the ship Harold had left the dock and left us with seventy-seven tons of peas, according to the shipworker. Bob, however, demanded payment for one hundred tons and got it, although the *Cambria* sailed to Mistley twenty-three tons short.

Dried peas held no great fascination for the dockers, a gang of whom were loading the *Cambria* with one hundred tons of the green "ball-bearings" just before Christmas, 1969. After their "mobile", dockology for lunch break, a derivative of the days when refreshment was supplied on four wheels, a lighter moored alongside the *Cambria* started loading tinned salmon. The word went round and even members of our gang swarmed over the barge's rails and into the lighter, where a "greenacre", a falling set of freight, was hastily arranged. The crane driver skilfully sought an accident; he bounced a set of boxes on the lighter's hatch coaming and our gang scrambled back aboard the *Cambria* with shirts stuffed full with tins of salmon.

With knives, nails and cargo hooks they started ripping open the tins and wolfing the contents. They threw the jagged empty cans into our cargo, and when we unloaded at Mistley we found them covered in green mould. However, they were a generous lot and one of the dockers handed me ten tins of the prize which I stowed below in the food locker.

Another time, one of our gang of dockers was sick after we had provided him with several requested cups of tea, which only whetted his appetite for one of the gallon tins of pineapple juice we were loading from a ship in the West India Dock.

To the lightermen the docks are huge boating ponds. There is no need to moor the dumb barges up properly, if at all, because they "can't go anywhere". It was not uncommon to see up to a dozen lighters all hanging off the "headfuss" (painter) of just one. More often than not lighters would roam free, lashed together in twos and threes, blowing around the dock with every wind change,

132

chased by the little "tosher" tugs when required for a ship. The dockers took great advantage of these "wild horses". Rather than a mile-long trek around the edge of a dock they would cast off a lighter and simply blow across to the other side like industrial windsurfers.

Another time in the Royal Victoria Dock I was over the side painting the wale when I heard the cry, "Oi, Picasso". Turning round I spotted a docker commuting in the time-honoured cavalier fashion. However, a sudden wind

Lighters and a tug alongside a Houlder liner in dock.

change was blowing the half-loaded lighter he was riding along the dock instead of across it. "Wot a lovely pitcher you're painting," he said. "Chuck us a line, can yer?"

Once in "the Tilbury", as the Tilbury Docks were colloquially known, Bob earned himself the name "Moby Dick" for clearing a brace of drifting lighters from our anchor with a long hitcher. "Cor, nice work, Moby," hollered one of our gang, "like ter see yer wiv a real 'arpoon."

Whatever else, you were always guaranteed a good crack in the docks.

During our busy working day in the docks I did not notice anything particularly anachronistic about the *Cambria*. It was only observation by a third party that brought home to me her antiquity. Did the cameramen from the National Maritime Museum actually know that a month after they had made their film of us in the West India Docks the *Cambria* would be out of commission?

During one of our freights of peas from the Royal Victoria Dock I was down in the hold sweeping the ceiling preparatory to loading. Bob was down aft. Two lorry drivers, unaware anyone was aboard, were discussing the barge. Perhaps the belief that they were alone encouraged them to express aloud their slightly uncertain speculation as to what the *Cambria* was. I heard a voice say: "Yeah, it's one of them galleons the pirates used to float round the oceans in."

The certainty that we must have an engine signalled a new breed of men who had never experienced dealing with barges. Once, as we were heaving the *Cambria* into the lock at the Tilbury Dock, one of the younger hands demanded that we "Stop". Just like that! Bob reached up for the mizzen sheets which ran over the top of the wheelhouse, tugged them twice and said in a loud voice, "Full astern."

To get our freights in the London River we were "fixed" by Ray Sully, who took ten per cent, which was also supposed to give us our "turn", but I can recall swinging round the buoy at Grays for three weeks without orders while barges arriving after us jumped the queue. This might have had something to do with 'phone calls made to Sully and the Board of Trade claiming that the *Cambria* was "unfit to carry cargo" as she was wetting every freight. This unpleasant and inaccurate piece of malice resulted in a surprise visit to the barge by a Board of Trade official who ordered canvas scuttle covers to be made, landing us with expensive and unnecessary delay.

Shortly after this Bob discovered time's tides were beginning to run against him from unexpected quarters. After 'phoning for orders one afternoon he returned to Grays causeway where I was tending to the boat. Looking rather crestfallen he passed on the comment Sully had made to him:

"Why don't you go and sail round the world?"

A typical sight! *Cambria* had been waiting at Grays buoy for orders for over a week; the motor barge *Phoenician* had just arrived, received orders and loaded grain at the terminal in the background, and was at the buoy for battening down and washing round before sailing for Maldon.   *Dick Durham*

CHAPTER EIGHTEEN

Rubicon in Halfway Reach

THE SHIP that Will built was making water and she was wetting cargoes, although only after a bad weather passage when deep loaded. Considering her keel was laid down in 1906, the *Cambria* was a credit to her builder. She had cost £1,895, just ten pounds more than the ship his brother Fred had built, the *Hibernia*, the *Cambria's* sister ship, which a north-easterly gale brought to a premature end. Her bones lie scattered along the Norfolk coast near Cromer.

We once took a hammering while deep-laden with 160 tons of wheat from Tilbury Terminal to Felixstowe. The *Cambria* made a considerable amount of water on that freight. The two pumps aft were of metal with back-breaker handles, as Bob called them. They were difficult to prime but threw a good deal more water than those amidships. The black bilge water poured over the side as we cranked away for half an hour morning and evening. We had to wait for three days for our berth at Marriage's mill in the dock.

I would listen intently for the sucking noise which announced that the *Cambria* was nearly dry. After some time at the pumps I would start to hallucinate, pretending to hear or feel the pumps sucking. However, when the time actually arrived there was no doubting it. The imagined time of sucking helped to boost morale and Bob and I would say to each other, "I think she's nearly done," when, in fact, she was far from done.

When the pumps had sucked aft we would go amidships and begin again. The wooden handles of those pumps were worn smooth and shiny by the horny hands of countless bargemen.

At Mistley the manager of the Ind Coope maltings once came down and complained about the smell emanating from our bilge water while I was pumping out. I noticed the swans fussing around the barge were pecking at the black stinky water for grain and peas. I told the man the smell was caused by the peas we were delivering for him to strain his beer mixing with our bilge water. He did not seem to want to hear any more about it.

During the *Cambria's* last six months in commission she had an engine. Bob bought a motor pump, the first, and only, internal combustion engine ever to grace the old barge.

As *Cambria's* grey and battered hull sailed in and out of the Thames Estuary rivers she passed the picture postcard sights of an ever increasing flotilla of yacht barges. Some of them had been rigged out according to the example of the last remaining working barge. Bob had a quiet chuckle at the zeal of those who had rigged out the *Thalatta*. He had spotted one of them making notes of the *Cambria's* bowsprit rigging. When the lofty *Thalatta* was eventually re-rigged her bowsprit stays were half cable, half chain, just like those on the *Cambria*. Yet the riggers on Everards' yard had made up the *Cambria's* stays that way simply because they had not enough cable. The chain had been pragmatically inserted to make up the length!

Another barge, the *May*, passed us once in the River Medway. Her skipper, Bob Wells, was a good bargeman who was earning a pleasant living sailing her round the coast for the management of Tate and Lyle to entertain clients aboard. The way her bowsprit rigging had been bent on made her look as though she were a trawler. As she sailed by Bob yelled out to his old friend, "Caught much?" Skipper Wells laughed, waved and shrugged in reply.

The yacht barges disappeared in the autumn, and at night on the London River we never saw them winter or summer. This went some way to explain the ignorance of a Port of London Authority launch skipper who bellowed through

Left: Ephraim Sharman dressed as the "mayor" of Pin Mill at the wedding of Bob Roberts' daughter Jill in June, 1970.

Opposite: The barges *Cambria* and *Royalty* towing into Yarmouth harbour behind the old paddle tug *United Service*.
Tony Farnham collection

a loud hailer at the *Cambria* one dark night, as she slipped by the garish lights of Thames Haven, "*Cambria*, ahoy, *Cambria* ahoy. A ship has complained about your sidelights, they're not bright enough. By the way, where's your masthead light?" Bob shouted back, "Sailing vessels don't have masthead lights. Go back to bloody school." He then ordered me to turn up the wicks in the port and starboard lights.

The *Cambria's* trading potential had shrunk drastically over her last years.

The barge had, in her heyday, carried freight anywhere between Goole and Exeter in Britain and to the ports between Bruges in Belgium, with wheat from London, and le Tréport in France, with coal from Keadby. As her age increased so did the restrictions made by the Board of Trade. By the late sixties the *Cambria's* limits were between Yarmouth and Dover, and during my time aboard they were reduced to between Ipswich and Dover.

One bright ray came in June, 1970, with the marriage of Bob's youngest daughter, Jill. The BBC were showing interest yet again in the old barge for a programme in a series of documentaries on disappearing rural life. The series, called *Look Stranger*, was filmed at Pin Mill and took in Jill's colourful wedding and reception at the *Butt and Oyster*.

Bob and I tacked the barge back and forth in the river for a couple of days in the early summer sunshine. I was to come out along the bowsprit end and furl the jib. The motorboat filming me was below the bow and out of Bob's vision. As a consequence he was calling for me to point to the craft while at the same time the film crew kept shouting, "Don't look at the camera".

We had some fun with the crew in the pub afterwards but several evenings running it was a trudge back up to Dwiny Cottage at closing time and, according to Bob, "home to a cold dinner and a warm reception". He reckoned he could always tell how late he was for dinner by the number of rings formed round the plate as the gravy shrank. "One ring per hour", he estimated. Briefly, but falsely, it was like the old days.

If it blew hard from the south or west invariably the *Cambria* would find a mooring in Gravesend Reach rather than at Grays in order to benefit from the shelter of a weather shore. One winter afternoon in 1969 or 1970 the *Cambria* lay alongside an empty lighter moored off Denton in Kent. We had orders to load one hundred tons of fishmeal from a ship in Surrey Commercial Docks. It was blowing a near gale from the south west. Bob cast off our stern line from the lighter, and as he did he fell heavily on to his elbow. When he got aboard he seemed for the first time to show his age. His face was grey and lined, and he looked very tired.

With tops'l, fores'l and just one cloth of mainsail set the *Cambria* thrashed up Gravesend Reach, lee rail awash and sidelights throwing flickering patterns on the grey water. It was six o'clock by the time we passed the Tilbury Ferry. Just two passengers stood on deck. In the lee of the wheelhouse, they watched us beat by from the comfort of their dufflecoat hoods. High water was at eleven o'clock that night and we had to be ready for the ship by 8.30 the following morning.

Dense rainsqualls hit the barge, making her sit over further. I stood under the meagre shelter of the mainmast wondering if the huge manacles clamping the sprit to the mast would part and crush me to pulp against the rigging. Points of light in the darkness ahead broke free to form the shapes of moving ships. In

Erith Rands a mighty squall dipped the *Cambria* down, rolling the barge poles into the scuppers. At the same time we heard a ripping sound. Looking aloft I could see a hole appearing in the mainsail. Bob put the helm up. "Get the mainsail in as we come about," he yelled. This I did and we continued beating across the head of one ship and under the stern of another until Halfway Reach. On the port tack and heading for a road of lighters moored under the neon signature of Mr Henry Ford's factory, Bob shouted, "Ready 'bout," and the *Cambria's* head started coming up into the wind. Then the wind suddenly headed us as it screamed across the black silhouetted outline of chimneys. The *Cambria* fell back on her course, racing towards the lighters. "Down tops'l, down anchor," Bob yelled as the wet shiny sides of the lighters loomed ever nearer. Both done, we slowed, stopped and came into the wind half a barge's length from the roads.

We set the tops'l again, and after helping to heave up the anchor I watched the flickering, wet, oilskinned figure of Bob running back to the wheel. The *Cambria* crossed the reach on starboard and as we came about the same thing happened again. This time she was carrying more way but lost it by the time she had come into the wind. We were in irons. The sails leaped, jumped and raged like pterodactyls on chains. She eventually fell over on to the port tack again but the squall had taken its toll. Looking aloft, I could see a three-foot rent in the tack of the tops'l. I ran aft and blurted this fact to Bob. Without looking at me he said, "I know." There was no order to drop the sail. Without it we could get no further towards our freight. In the next minute such considerations became academic.

With a bang and a crack the gale jumped through the tops'l like a circus lion through a paper skin. Bits of topsail blew away into the night, some the size of

Opposite: *Cambria* in Halfway Reach.

Right: The blown-out topsail.
Dick Durham

Penny, Bob Roberts and the author in *Cambria's* cabin while lying at Erith for repairs in March, 1970.
Kentish Times

bats, others like flying carpets. In place of our tops'l glowed with mocking irony the Ford sign.

We gybed the *Cambria* round and under fores'l alone sailed back to a buoy in Erith Reach with the tatters of the tops'l like so many ribbons in the wind. The London and Rochester barge *Rock*, skippered by Jimmy Didhams and with Steve Mallett as mate, motored past us bound up river. The gale was no obstacle to them. Suddenly it all seemed absurd. The *Cambria* was beyond her time.

The British Oil and Cake Mills at Erith generously gave us a fine chalk "campshed" berth at their wharves free of charge while we got another topsail. Bob managed to get one from Everards'. He had sailed under it before; it once belonged to the *Dreadnought*.

While we were repairing the damage a reporter and photographer from the

Erith Observer and Kentish Thames arrived. They were surprised to see a fire blazing in the saloon. "On a wooden boat and all, you'd a thought it would have caught alight, like," said the photographer. He then asked Bob if he would don oilskins to pose at the wheel for a picture. This terminated the interview. "What do you want me to look like, an advertisement for fish paste?" Bob asked.

From 2nd February to 19th April the *Cambria* underwent a complete overhaul. We shifted down river to Grays once we had bent on the new topsail and lowered down to get the mainsail repaired.

John "Ginger" Calver provided the barge with brand new topmast stays. He had once sailed with Bob as third hand on the *Greenhithe*. Now as a rigger working at major oil refineries he remembered his skipper in the best possible tradition!

Bob detested anyone suggesting he was doing anything out of the ordinary. As a schoolboy I would come home on cold winter nights and, with my telescope, scan the *Cambria's* yellow riding light as she lay in the West Leigh Middle bound either up or down river. With that little yellow glow in my imagination I would switch off the electric light and climb into my warm bed thinking of the cold, isolated, crew of the barge laying out in the river. I told Bob about this and how it made me feel even cosier tucked up in bed. "We were just as cosy out on the barge," he retorted.

In London River and elsewhere we were sometimes visited by missionaries from the Flying Angel, the Missions to Seamen, to make sure Bob had not got me in chains and living on bread crusts. One who came aboard at Ipswich wanted me to read a handful of ecclesiastical literature while he sat and waited. I deduced he was just nosy and asked him to leave. Another came aboard while we were once in the West India Docks and advertised the fact that the Canning Town Seamen's Mission was holding a Saturday night dance.

"You'll be all right," he winked, "the girls get in free of charge on the condition they don't refuse a dance to anyone." It seemed to me they saw us as freaks who could not operate socially.

In the main, the overtaking motor barges were friendly towards the old *Cambria*. Many offered her a tow in calm weather, but the odd bargeman showed a grudge against Bob. Dave Kennard remembers one such time when the *Cambria* was close-hauled in Gravesend Reach and a motor barge overhauled her under her lee, forcing Bob to luff the barge.

Dave said: "Bob deliberately let *Cambria* thump the motor barge on the quarter and he shouted at the skipper, 'You've had some of this, you ought to know better.' I should have hated to have crossed him."

One, more amusing, side of Bob's old-fashioned ways I experienced myself one night when sailing up Sea Reach. I was at the wheel. Bob was below eating his supper. When he came on deck he asked me, "Who's Jimi Hendrix?"

"An American pop star. Why?"

"Oh, is he? Well, he's dead." Bob had heard it on the BBC news. "That's one less who'll sing of being in lurv."

As he took the wheel I looked up river trying to imagine a starker contrast—Bob Roberts and a man who played an electric guitar with his mouth.

After the *Cambria's* refit we started the long wait for freights once again. Bob wondered what he would do with the *Cambria*; her end as a commercial trader was very near. He asked me if I could help him sail her out "into the middle of the North Sea" and sink her. I said I would. For a time Bob considered this seriously. He told me we could use a high-powered motorcraft in which to return. There were some more freights yet to come. We took peas to Mistley, wheat to Stambridge Mills at Rochford, groundnut cake to Colchester and Ipswich. It was to Ipswich that the *Cambria* carried her last freight.

Bob had already started negotiations with the newly-formed Maritime Trust, set up to preserve historic ships, when on Thursday, 15th October, 1970, we loaded one hundred tons of cattle cake from the ss *Falaba* at No 32 berth in Tilbury Docks.

Old habits die hard. Before we left Grays buoy to load the last freight we heard that an old steam tug lying alongside was to be scrapped. Immediately we scoured the engine room for coal and topped up several sacks which we gingerly lifted across the road of lighters between us and the tug. As the lighters clanged together, rattling their batten hooks in the swell from passing ships, we swung the sacks aboard.

We completed loading on the Friday and came out of Tilbury Dock on Saturday afternoon, bringing up at the bottom end of the Lower Hope. The next morning a west-north-westerly wind carried us as far as the south-east Maplin where it westered. We lowered the bowsprit and carried our sail to Butterman's Bay.

Tuesday saw us unloading at Eastern Counties Farmers' wharf at Ipswich. The dockers chased a rat around the hold but it jumped over the side, inviting many obvious remarks.

On Wednesday the Crescent Shipping motor barge *Cecil Gilders* towed us into the lock where the *Cambria's* port leeboard jammed under the outer lock gate as it opened. The keeper said he could not remember such a thing happening in fifty years. As the *Cecil Gilders* reversed we hauled astern on the crab winch, but that did no good. We swung out the sprit and the lock hands swung on the vang. It was still no use, the *Cambria* obviously did not want to leave. Eventually we levered the leeboard clear with a long iron bar. The last entry in *Cambria's* cargo book reads: "Oct 22 (3 pm) Sailed light from Ipswich for London. Arrived London (Gravesend) 5 pm."

Uncharacteristically Bob had omitted to insert the arrival date at Gravesend, 23rd October. The last line on the page perhaps explains his oversight.

"Barge laid up—out of commission."

CHAPTER NINETEEN

Into Power

T HE HATCHES were cluttered with ropes, ladders, shovels and setting booms. All the paraphernalia of a sailing merchantman. Bob stood silently coiling down a line. Almost by habit, he slowly built a circle of rope from the left to the right. It was difficult for him to believe there was no point. All the years he had been barging he had been fit. The thick strong arms now seemed redundant, the barrel chest just something ungainly that spoilt the hang of shore-going clothes.

Now, without the barge, a dread of age crept over him. Toni had had a heart attack. It was a melancholy reminder of his span.

Jill said: "He was terrified of illness. He couldn't stand it when Mummy had a heart attack."

Bob developed bronchitis. Soon after, he had a severe car crash in his MG Magnette. It shook him up badly. The *Cambria* was sold to the Maritime Trust. Bob received £5,000.

I was offered a job at £35 a week, six times the pay I had earned as mate of the *Cambria*, to remain as a rigger/caretaker aboard, but after we sailed the barge to Upnor on the River Medway, where she was to lie, I left. Bob shook my hand and said, "We won't make a fuss about this because I'll be seeing you."

Bob stayed behind. He was to take the barge on a "tour" of east coast ports on behalf of the Trust to promote the Trust's aim of preserving old ships. The BBC went along as well, in the form of Fyfe Robertson, who was to do a radio broadcast on the old barge's last voyage.

When the order came down from Admiral Bailey, chairman of the Maritime Trust, that the red ensign must be struck every night at sunset, Bob said to Bert, "I've heard it all now."

The Trust employed shipwrights to survey the barge and it was discovered that her bottom was riddled with worm. She was carved up and new bottom boards were put in. Bert said: "You don't take planks out of a barge's bottom; they're rabbeted. You double 'em but you don't take them out. They put these new planks in and after that you could hear the water roaring out of her bottom when she dried out." His son, Ken, was taken on and paid £10 a day to fit new vangs and other rigging. A staircase in parana pine was built into the hold. It cost £300.

Bob's mind wandered over the past. He was at a loss what to do next. He remembered old Tom, the cook aboard the Everard ship *Capacity*, whom we had met at Felixstowe. While his ship was discharging, the young crew had gone off home to their families. Old Tom's family had all grown up and gone. His sight was not good enough to enable him to stand a watch and he had drifted back afloat in the galley of an old coaster. He drank alone until we arrived. So glad was he of our company that he made us a first-class breakfast aboard the ship the following morning. At lunchtime he wanted us to go off to the pub with him again. We left the dock that day. It was some weeks later when we heard old Tom had drowned in the harbour. Apparently, coming back from the pub one night he had slipped.

According to Jill, Bob always used to say he was born in 1906. "He liked to think of himself as being the same age as the barge. When she was sold the whole edifice had gone. He was never the same."

When his wife died, Bob became very morose. He began to consider his own end. How long would it be? Had he really finished his own life with the *Cambria's* demise?

He remembered his father's death in 1944. It had been quick. In an armchair after lunch. Bob told Cis: "He was damn lucky. I only hope when my time comes, I go like that, just like a candle."

A woman was to change many attitudes in Bob's late years, a woman he had met many years earlier at the Erith Yacht Club. Sheila Blackburn was just a little girl when she watched the rough, rugged bargeman rolling along the towpath. She had never forgotten him, and their paths had crossed on and off through the years.

He had always held a sneaking admiration for the wilful young woman who had sailed her boyfriend's yacht, the *Torcello*, a German prize from the war, single-handed from Cubitts Basin in London to Cowes. She had also helped Bob sail the yacht *Chica* back from Holland after Toni had broken her rib. Now, with a broken marriage behind her, Sheila visited the *Cambria*, which had been opened to the public. "Here was this moping ship-keeper envious of two scruffy young lads going aboard a Crescent Shipping coaster. He thought he would take his place on the old bench at Pin Mill where all the other skippers before him had sat, and keep moving up till he fell off the end."

Sheila convinced Bob that he must go back to sea.

It was all Bob needed. A year after the *Cambria* carried her last freight he bought the 260-ton motor coaster *Vectis Isle*. His enemies took delight in scoffing

Cambria off Silvertown during her last trip to London before being handed over to the Maritime Trust. Her bowsprit is steeved up and the mizzen brailed up.
Tony Farnham collection

145

at the last sailorman going into power, but Sheila put it the best way on behalf of those who thought otherwise: "Taking the *Vectis Isle* was the bravest thing he ever did. At his age, facing his critics and taking on something completely strange took a lot of courage."

Bob took delivery of his new ship in September, 1971. She cost £11,000.

In the early days Bob was "like a monkey who'd found a space-ship", according to an old friend, the author and broadcaster John Seymour. When another motorship skipper, ex-bargeman Paddy O'Donnell, first met up with the *Vectis Isle* at Newport, Isle of Wight, he had to explain gently to Bob, as he used

Sheila Roberts aboard the motor coaster *Vectis Isle*.

Mrs Sheila Roberts

springs to warp her astern, that he actually had engines with which to reverse! "He thought he was still in the barge," said Paddy.

Astonished crews of passing coasters tuned in on their VHF radios to hear Bob being given a guide to the engine room and its procedures over the air. As he learned the complexities of the machinery, helpful skippers could be heard saying, "Now face the engine. On your left hand you have the oil pump . . ."

Sheila said: "We tried to get qualified engineers, but it was difficult. They were away deep sea or in a garage. We couldn't pay the big money."

Sheila and Bob married and bought a house in Ryde, Isle of Wight, to be near Newport where most of their freights were fixed by Carisbrooke Shipping. His second wife became mate, cook and deckhand on many passages. Finding and keeping reliable crew proved a nightmare. The Wage and Share Book from September, 1971, until November, 1974, reads like a marine probation officer's log. In that period ten mates or deckhands deserted ship, three were dismissed because of "drunkenness" and two were discharged owing to "ill health".

When they eventually found a reliable engineer, Ernie Young, he still had to turn for help from foreign colleagues because the engine manual was in Dutch.

Sheila said that they could hear the dockers banging on the side of the ship in the morning and they would wait and see if the crew would muster and uncover. "Nothing would happen so we'd go on deck and start taking the hatches off ourselves."

Once the sound of the banging hatches had brought the crew on deck, Bob would round on them saying, "If my missus is heaving hatchboards, why aren't you? I'll get a nursemaid for you." Hoping for any "extra" work was impossible. Bob would threaten his crew with "a gang from ashore" to do the chipping and painting required, but it was all in vain.

Bob started approaching his old shipmates. Fred "Bimbo" Mackie was out collecting lobster pots one morning when he noticed a familiar figure standing on Margate pierhead. When he got ashore it was Bob inquiring if he would be interested in a berth. "He told me he wanted a mate but he wanted more than that. He wanted someone to take her so he could stop ashore." Fred told Bob that his days at sea were over. He was content with his pots.

Sheila even sounded out Jimmy Uglow one Christmas when Bob was stuck for a mate. Jimmy said "He'd got a nerve if nothing else."

I managed a couple of freights, china clay from Charlestown in Cornwall to Queenborough in Kent and barley from Newport, Isle of Wight, to Ipswich.

His old friend, Jack Govier, a retired brigadier, who remembered the hard old times aboard the *Martinet* when they used to remove a panel in the bulkhead to fill it with wheat to distribute to Pin Mill chicken keepers, was another who crewed aboard *Vectis Isle*. So too was Jerry Thomason.

Fortunately during January, 1975, Bob had a mate who hailed from the Essex village of Mistley, famous for producing a long line of excellent seamen. That was Jim Finch. He and Ernie Young gave Bob a welcome relief from the inferior hands he had had to put up with.

It was fortunate because during that month of January *Vectis Isle* came through some of the worst weather that Bob ever experienced in her. Early on the morning of the 25th the little coaster was rolling in heavy seas off Portland Bill on passage from Dean Quarry near Falmouth to Cowes with 262 tons of granite chippings. The glass had fallen rapidly and the light westerly wind that had seen them clear of the Manacles had grown into a full gale from the south-west by the time they had reached the Bill.

Sheila was aboard and remembers that gale. "Bob, Jim and Ernie all remained in the wheelhouse. I can remember Ernie being at the wheel while Bob kept giving course corrections, sometimes to just a quarter of a degree, to keep the wind right behind us. Ernie quietly repeated each course. Because of water on deck I could not leave the dayroom to get to the galley and make them any hot food."

Sheila simply held Penny to stop the hound rolling from side to side and listened to the concentrated voices of *Vectis Isle's* crew coming through an access hatch.

To their horror, at 06.22 GMT they picked up a Mayday on the VHF. It was from the doomed ship *Lovat* twenty-five miles south of Land's End. Her cargo of washed anthracite dust had liquefied, formed a slurry and given the ship a ten-degree list. As the hours went by they all listened intently to the rescue operation. The Penlee lifeboat was launched and a Sea King helicopter hovered over the frothing rollers.

Sheila was no stranger to heavy weather. She had made long passages delivering yachts in her youth. She had been across the Bay of Biscay en route to Gibraltar when a westerly gale had made the craft fight for her passage. And on another voyage to the Baltic she had been storm-tossed while helping take a large ketch to Sweden. But she never forgot that night aboard the *Vectis Isle*.

"The fo'c'sle was only just visible above the seas. Wedges kept washing from the hatch coamings, and some straps across the hatch cloths parted. I remember once I'd asked Bob if he would tell me when he thought the weather was bad."

Bob did not tell Sheila of his fears during the passage, but he was worried that his ship's hatches would burst.

"I passed the lads some beer and biscuits, which was all there was in the dayroom. It was very frightening."

Abreast the Needles the ship's log recalls: "Very rough seas, cannot see land or buoys. Must go round outside the Island." Two and a half hours later the log records: "Off St Catherines, SW 10. Continually swept." Eventually when they got some lee off Sandown Bob turned to Sheila and said: "You remember you wanted to know when it was bad weather? Well that was bad. Now let's have some food."

Four and a half hours later *Vectis Isle* was moored safely at Medina Wharf, Cowes.

"The wharfhands said I still looked white as a sheet," says Sheila.

For the crew of the *Lovat* the weather proved too much. She rolled over and sank, and only two of her thirteen crew survived. Ironically, one of the ships that went to her assistance, the *Nimrod*, also rolled over and sank two years later off Cromer when her cargo shifted. Like *Vectis Isle* she was loaded with granite chippings.

Sheila remained at home when the ship "went foreign" in order to look after Penny. Strict quarantine regulations prevented the hound going to the Continent, though occasionally Bob ignored them.

At one time in Rotterdam Bob had to fly home to get his passport which he had forgotten. There was an IRA scare and he fitted the description of the wanted terrorist. Bob's first experience of air travel caused him to comment: "I was full of excitement at the airport, but to the people around me it was as though we were catching a bus."

The light moments were few and far between as crew problems mounted. Once at Brussels Bob had to rescue his mate who had got drunk. Bob wrote to Sheila about the affair: "Found him rotten drunk in a cafe and owing a bill of 335 francs. I paid this, got a taxi and took him back to the ship, about 9 pm. At 10 pm he recovered, crept ashore and went back to the same cafe, still very drunk. Got a taxi again and got him back to the ship and into his bunk. It is now 9 am and he is still there, fully clothed. He was a pitiful sight last night. I will have to keep him short of money."

Ernie, the engineer, helped Bob keep his chin up. Once, taking a pilot up the River Maas to Rotterdam, the Dutchman asked for a sandwich. They had only cheese aboard but the man insisted on a "flesh" sandwich. All Ernie could find

The *Vectis Isle* in the Channel Islands in the nineteen-seventies.   *Mrs Sheila Roberts*

Arthur "Bully" Bull sailing in the River Stour, 1982.
The late Arthur Bull

was a tin of dog food. The pilot swallowed the lot, unaware it was anything other than meat for human consumption.

The *Vectis Isle* traded fairly regularly to Mistley, to where Bob had sailed many times in the barges. On one trip she developed trouble with her anchor winch. Bob inquired if there was an engineer in the village. One of the wharf hands said a Mr Bull lived up the hill, retired but a good mechanic.

"Not Arthur Bull by any chance?" asked Bob. "Don't know, but it's three Rigby Road," came the reply.

Bob trudged up the hill, his heart in his mouth. When the door opened there stood the greying but unmistakable chunky frame of Bully. Bully burst into tears and the men embraced.

All the years that had passed since their last meeting had not erased the memories of Bob's stubbornness over engines and Bully's frustrated expertise aboard the *Thelma*. Bob smiled wryly and asked Bully if he could employ him to repair the winch. Before the ship left Mistley it was working better than it had ever done before.

Another time the *Vectis Isle* was coming away from Maldon. The ancient town had become the Mecca of yacht-barges. There was not a soul aboard the barges along Hythe Quay who did not know the owner of the little Dutch ship as she motored past. Suddenly it was as though everybody had something to do. The young hands on the barges were squinting aloft or coiling down. But what was this? Bob Roberts actually waving at them? All eyes swung towards the grey ship. Yes, he was definitely waving. All hands returned the greeting. None of them had spotted Sheila in the road behind waving goodbye to her outward bound husband!

At seventy, Bob was getting too old to stand long tricks at the wheel but poor quality mates were forcing him to spend even longer at the helm than he had ever done on the barge. The *Vectis Isle* was running regularly to the Continent and down channel to Cornish ports and the Channel Islands. During one voyage from Bow Creek in London to Caen, France, with scrap Bob was relieved only once and that was for only two hours.

He wrote to Sheila: "As might be expected, the crew were tired out before we started and it was difficult to get any of them out of their bunks. The mate is pretty hopeless. He puts me in mind of a doughnut with whiskers on. Initiative nil, energy nil, comprehension nil—just a doughnut! He came on watch two hours late and then I had to stay with him while he steered, traffic being thick in the Channel."

Bob never gave up hope in trying to find a good mate.

He wrote: "Started teaching Brian to steer but his eyes are very bad and he needs glasses. But at least he tries and is interested. I think I might eventually make something of him." A mate who did shine was Andrew Colquhourn, who was with Bob for two and a half years. Initially Bob was a little prickly with Andrew's "hippy" ways but soon realised they were only superficial.

Unfortunately Andrew left and Bob was back with experiences of drunkenness and an insidious new vice—drug-taking. He decided he had had enough. Not only was he having to suffer appalling crews but also the ship was out-of-date and too small to pay for the three hands she required plus engine repairs which were astronomical. It was not like splicing up a new sheet.

In a sad letter home to Sheila he decided it all.

"Tom the 'mate' and Terry went off on the booze last night and God knows what else. At 11 o'clock the mission bus brought me back but they would not come. Next morning they were found in Ghent (about 12 miles away) very drunk. Tom had been beaten up and left lying on the pavement outside a bar. His face is in a dreadful mess.

"Somehow they were got to the Seamen's Mission in Ghent about 8 am apparently both hopeless. The Ghent mission let them sleep on settees for a while and phoned the Terneuzen mission. The Terneuzen chap was kind enough to take his own car to Ghent and bring them back to the ship. The whole episode disgusts me.

"Sheila dear, I have just about had a bellyful of crew troubles augmenting ship troubles."

Bob even remembered Ephraim's old one-liner to Sheila: "Everything in our favour's against us." He wrote: "I shall make a serious effort to sell the ship."

His last freight was 260 tonnes of cement from Shoreham to Newport, Isle of Wight.

After 301 cargoes in the *Vectis Isle*, Bob put her on the market in February, 1978.

He came ashore for good.

CHAPTER TWENTY

Understanding the Past

T HE TURQUOISE and white ferry headed straight for the breakfast table; her red and black funnel in line with her sharp stem was disappearing behind a corn flake packet.

Before she was hull down beneath the cereal box, she turned hard to port and left her wash to swish on in and break at the foot of Bob's garden. I sat in the morning room of St Anne's Cottage admiring the panoramic view which took in the bustle of the Ryde–Portsmouth ferry.

"They must line up your cottage for their turning point," I said to Bob.

He grunted, threw a reluctant stare towards the disappearing ferry and said, "They'll be on strike soon."

He passed me *The Daily Telegraph* and tapped a column reporting on a planned National Union of Seamen's strike. To Bob anyone calling himself a seaman who was prepared to cut off an island was a betrayer of his profession.

Yet the strike was not surprising; just the way things were going.

Bob was seventy-three years old and not interested in hearing of my visit to the *Cambria* at her new berth in London's St Katharine's Dock. Her spars, without sails, were like stark winter trees. Somebody had painted her anchor black. It seemed to signify the rather frivolous way in which she had been "preserved". In her hold sat two dusty dummies in historical dress. They formed part of an *Onedin Line* exhibition, a television story of a nineteenth-century Liverpool shipping family. Bob had been a "technical advisor" for the series.

I began to mention that part of the barge's ceiling had been removed and a pump installed but he cut me short and changed the subject.

"Went trawling in the whaler yesterday," he said. "Got two dabs, a plimsoll and a turd." He laughed and drove me down to the *Folly Inn*, situated on a fine sheltered part of the River Medina. Here Bob kept his twenty-five-foot whaler rigged with a gunter mainsail and foresail.

Upriver lay an Everard coaster at the cement wharf. It was Paddy O'Donnell's ship, but he was not aboard and the mate did not know how to

Captain Bob Roberts at the wheel of the *Cambria*.
BBC photograph

operate the mechanical hatches, which made Bob give up the idea of getting a sack of cement to fill the cracks in his garage wall. We motored downriver to Cowes, passing a scabrous Baltic ketch with hardboard, larger-than-life-size pirates leaping in the wind from the rigging. Bob looked at me, then raised his eyebrows heavenwards.

Three people braved the biting wind to wave away the ferry from Ryde Pier when I left the island. Bob was one of them. Watching a seaman let go aft he said loudly at him *via* me, "Make the most of it, Dick; they're going on strike soon." Whether or not the crewman was suitably humbled was impossible to tell from his blank expression, but like Captain Bligh, Bob was not going to be cast adrift on the Isle of Wight without saying something about it. To him a seamen's strike was a mass mutiny.

The ferry pulled away. I watched Bob getting smaller, walking to his car and raising his hand to make Penny jump. I never saw him again.

During his last years ashore Bob suffered dreadful nightmares. On moonlit nights, silent nights, when only the wash of the tide could be heard on the beach, Bob would suddenly shout in his sleep. Sheila would wake him and alone, as they sat in bed in the dark, sketchy details of Bob's wartime experiences would leak out from him. Once calmed he would go back to sleep and in the mornings nothing was ever said. Sheila would have to wait until the next nightmare before learning more.

To some mates and friends, including myself, Bob mentioned that he had been involved with secret boat landings in occupied France, Holland and Belgium. Bill Everard was in charge of the Coastal Section of the Ministry of Shipping during the 1939–45 conflict. It seems likely that it was through his boss that Bob volunteered for these missions which were to land saboteurs/agents in occupied countries or to retrieve escaping airmen. On one trip Bob took a motorship to spike the guns at Dunkirk after the evacuation. The ship was hit and many men were lost. One crewman lost his mind as the vessel limped home and he was admitted to Stone psychiatric hospital near Dartford, Kent.

On another occasion German troops opened fire on Bob's party. Bob escaped with his life, but others died; the dying men called out to Bob, thinking him a traitor. They felt he had double-crossed them. He never recovered from this appallingly incorrect stigma. Only at night and to Sheila did such mysterious and baffling bits and pieces come out. "He would wake up yelling, with tears rolling down his cheek. His face seemed to go flat, leaden. His eyes would be bolting out of his head. I think it was terror. It was dreadful, fearful. He was in extreme distress."

Bob went to visit a survivor at the Stone hospital, but he refused to talk.

Sheila said: "Bob could see nothing but hate in the man's eyes. He just wanted him out of his sight."

Bob's daughter, Anne, also remembers her mother talking of Bob's return after the Dunkirk trip: "He was shaking from head to toe, my mother told me. It shook her up, too. She'd never seen him like that."

Bob kept his agony a secret. To everyone on the Isle of Wight he was a friendly, amusing man, great company and very active with the squeezebox. He appeared at the Royal Albert Hall and the Royal Festival Hall in concerts arranged by the English Folk Dance and Song Society.

Many other old shipmates visited him. Jack Govier, a friend from Erith days, had become very close, especially after discovering Bob was a fellow mason. Bob had been initiated in May, 1936, at St Cuthberga Lodge, number 622 at Wimborne. His father, a past Master, had introduced Bob at the age of twenty-eight to the order. When Bob moved he joined St Luke's Lodge, number 225 at Ipswich. Both Jack and Ron Turner cited Bob for the OBE, which he failed to get.

Another regular visitor was John Dickens, who once joined Bob on a visit to his father's grave near Wimborne. Bob kneeled in the soft earth, grunting, as he planted bulbs in his father's memory. He turned and said to John,

"You cannot understand the present unless you understand the past."

*   *   *

The brow of the hill swallowed Sheila's car and Bob lowered his hands back to the steering of the bicycle. It was beginning to feel like hard work, pushing up the hill. He started to pant.

Farmer's wife Marion Corney took little interest in the elderly man gliding past her kitchen window on his bicycle. She lifted her plate of food from the table and moved across the room to the comfortable chair. She liked it there; you could see up the hill from the side window.

When Bob toppled over, Mrs Corney thought another member of the Conservative Club had enjoyed a good lunch. When he did not get up, she went to call her husband.

Sheila wondered why Bob had not yet arrived at Arthur's home. She decided to drive back over the hill to see where he had got to. Down the lane in front of her a circle of people were standing in the road. There was a figure lying on his back.

The rear wheel of the bicycle was still ticking round.

Bibliography

Cooper, F. *Racing Sailormen.* Percival Marshall, 1963.

Roberts, A. W. *A Slice of Suffolk.* Terence Dalton, 1978.
   Breeze for a Bargeman. Terence Dalton, 1981.
   Coasting Bargemaster. Edward Arnold, 1949; Mallard Reprints, 1984.
   Last of the Sailormen. Routledge and Kegan Paul, 1960.
   Rough and Tumble. Sampson Low and Marston, 1935; Mallard Reprints, 1983.

Uglow, J. *Sailorman: A bargemaster's story.* Conway Maritime Press, 1975.

Winchester, C. (ed) *Shipping Wonders of the World.* Amalgamated Press.

Periodicals
Coast and Country. Parrett and Neves.
Daily Express.
Daily Mail.
East Coast Digest. Parrett and Neves.
English Dance and Song. The English Folk Dance and Song Society.
Erith Observer and Kentish Times.
Fishing News.
The Whitstable Times.

Index

Index of Barges and Ships